The old-time pamphlet ethos is back, with some of the most challenging work being done today. Prickly Paradigm Press is devoted to giving serious authors free rein to say what's right and what's wrong about their disciplines and about the world, including what's never been said before. The result is intellectuals unbound, writing unconstrained and creative texts about meaningful matters.

> "Long live Prickly Paradigm Press.... Long may its flaming pamphlets lift us from our complacency."
> —Ian Hacking

Prickly Paradigm is marketed and distributed by The University of Chicago Press.

www.press.uchicago.edu

A list of current and future titles can be found on our website and at the back of this pamphlet.

www.prickly-paradigm.com

Executive Publisher
Marshall Sahlins

Publishers
Peter Sahlins
Ramona Naddaff
Bernard Sahlins
Seminary Co-op Bookstore

Editor
Matthew Engelke
info@prickly-paradigm.com

David Hahn, Editorial Assistant
Design and layout by Bellwether Manufacturing.

The Inconstancy of the Indian Soul

The Inconstancy of the Indian Soul:
The Encounter of Catholics and Cannibals in 16th-Century Brazil

Eduardo Viveiros de Castro

Translated by Gregory Duff Morton

PRICKLY PARADIGM PRESS
CHICAGO

© 2011 Eduardo Viveiros de Castro.
All rights reserved.

Prickly Paradigm Press, LLC
5629 South University Avenue
Chicago, Il 60637

www.prickly-paradigm.com

ISBN: 978-0-984-2010-1-3
LCCN: 2011912027

Printed in the United States of America on acid-free paper.

Translation note

This pamphlet is a translation of a work that has been published several times—initially, as:

CASTRO, Eduardo B. Viveiros de, "O mármore e a murta: sobre a inconstância da alma selvagem", *Revista de Antropologia*. São Paulo, 35;21-74, 1992.

The translation was prepared based on a version that the author revised in 2010. It therefore departs, in certain small matters, from the previously-published editions.

Complete references for this pamphlet are available online at www.prickly-paradigm.com.

I
The Problem of Unbelief
in the Brazilian 16th Century

In a magnificent page of the *Sermon of the Holy Spirit* (1657), the Jesuit Antônio Vieira, one of the greatest figures of the Ibero-American baroque, wrote:

> You who have traveled through the world, and have entered into the pleasure-houses of princes, will have seen on those lawns and along those garden-paths two very different types of statues, those of marble and those of myrtle. The marble statue is quite difficult to make, because of the hardness and resistance of the material; but, once the statue has been fashioned, one no longer needs to put one's hand to it again: it always conserves and sustains the same shape. The statue of myrtle is easier to form, because of the ease with which the branches are bent, but one

must always keep reshaping it and working on it in order for it to stay the same. If the gardener ceases to pay attention, in four days a branch sticks out that runs through the statue's eyes, another one jumbles its ears, two more turn its five fingers into seven, and that which shortly before was a man is now a green confusion of myrtle. Here, then, lies the difference between some nations and others in the doctrine of faith. Some nations are naturally hard, tenacious, and constant, and with difficulty they receive the faith and leave behind the errors of their ancestors; they resist with arms, they doubt with their understanding, they repel with their will, they close themselves, they fear, they argue, they object, they take up much effort before they give themselves over; but, once they have given themselves over, once they have received the faith, they stay firm and constant in it, like statues of marble: it is no longer necessary to work with them. There are other nations, however—and such are those of Brazil—that receive everything that is taught them with great docility and ease, without arguing, without objecting, without doubting, without resisting. But they are statues of myrtle that, if the gardener lifts his hand and his scissors, will soon lose their new form, and return to the old natural brutishness, becoming a thicket as they were before. It is necessary for the teacher of these statues to attend to them always: at one point, to cut that which blooms in their eyes, so that they may believe what they do not see; at another, to uproot that which blooms in their ears, so that they do not listen to the fancies of their ancestors; at another, to sever that which blooms on their feet, so that they may abstain from the barbarous actions and habits of heathens. It is only in this way, working always against the nature of the trunk and the disposition

of the roots, that one can maintain these rude plants
in an unnatural shape, and the branches composed.

The "emperor of the Portuguese language," as Fernando
Pessoa called him, waxes eloquent here on a venerable
topic in the Jesuit literature about Indians. The theme
can already be found at the very beginning of the activities of the Society of Jesus in Brazil, in 1549, and a
single sentence sums it up: the natives of the land were
exasperatingly difficult to convert. Not because they
were made of refractory and intractable material—
on the contrary, they avidly sought new forms, but
seemed incapable of allowing themselves to be indel-
ibly impressed. A people receptive to any shape but
impossible to keep in one shape, the Indians—to use a
simile less European than the myrtle statue—were like
the forest that sheltered them, always ready to regain
the spaces precariously conquered by cultivation. They
were like their land, deceptively fertile, a place where it
appeared that anything could be planted, but where no
shoot sprouted without getting suffocated forthwith by
weeds. This people with no Faith, no Law, and no King
did not seem to offer a psychological and institutional
ground in which the Gospel might take root.

("Without faith, without law, without king"—"sem fé,
sem lei, sem rei"—makes a rhyming trio in Portuguese,
and served as common colonial shorthand for the state
of the native peoples of coastal Brazil, whose languages
did not feature the three initial phonemes of those
Portuguese words, /f/, /l/, and /r/). T. N.)

A.-C. Taylor has observed that the Indians of tropical
America were naturalized, above all, in the terms of

the vegetable kingdom. To cite an example that she does not use, see the contrast drawn by Gilberto Freyre between the "mineral resistance" of the Inca and Aztecs—the metaphor here is bronze, not marble—and the resistance of the Brazilian savages, "a pure vegetable sensibility or contractility." It would be worthwhile to trace the history of this imagery, which sometimes, as on Vieira's lips, irresistibly recalls Arcimboldo's compositions.

Among the pagans of the Old World, the missionary knew what resistances would have to be overcome: idols and priests, liturgies and theologies—religions worthy of the name, although rarely as exclusivist as the missionary's Christianity. In Brazil, on the other hand, the word of God was eagerly welcomed with one ear and negligently ignored with the other. Here, the enemy was not a different dogma, but an indifference to dogma, a refusal to choose. Inconstancy, disinterest, forgetfulness: "the people of these lands is the most brutish, the most ungrateful, the most inconstant, the most contrary, the most difficult to teach of all those in all the world," ranted and raved the disillusioned Vieira. This was why Christ designated Saint Thomas to preach in Brazil: it served as proper punishment for the apostle of doubt, this labor of bringing belief to those incapable of believing. Or capable of believing in everything, which amounts to the same: "Other peoples are unbelieving until they believe; the Brazilians, even after they have come to believe, are unbelieving."

Il selvaggio è mobile, then. The theme of Amerindian inconstancy had widespread success, both inside and outside of missionary discourse, and well beyond its initial case in point, the coastal Tupinambá.

Serafim Leite, the historian of the Society of Jesus in Brazil, relied on the observations of the first catechists and identified "deficiency of will" and "superficiality of feelings" as the primary obstacles to the conversion of the Indians. But he also drew from the opinions of laypeople, some of them quite distant from the Jesuits: Gabriel Soares de Souza, Alexandre Rodrigues Ferreira, Capistrano de Abreu, all unanimous in pointing out the amorphous nature of the savage soul.

This proverbial inconstancy was not observed only in matters of faith. In fact, it became a defining feature of the Amerindian character, consolidating itself as one of the stereotypes in the national imaginary: the half-converted Indian who, at the first opportunity, sends God, the hoe, and clothing to the devil, happily returning to the jungle, prisoner of an incurable atavism. Inconstancy is a constant in the savage equation.

> Serafim Leite could have also cited Gandavo: "They are very inconstant and changeable: they quickly believe everything that you persuade them to believe, no matter how troublesome and impossible, and then after any effort to dissuade them, they easily come to deny it..." Or he might also have turned to the anecdote of Léry's that concludes "Voilà l'Inconstance de ce pauvre peuple, bel example de la nature corrompue de l'homme..." ["Behold the inconstancy of this poor people, a fine example of the corrupt nature of man..."]. Abbeville, if I am not mistaken, was the only one to disagree, with an almost suspicious-sounding optimism: "Others say that they are inconstant, flighty. In truth they are inconstant, if allowing oneself to be guided only by reason may be called 'inconstancy,' but they are amenable to reasonable arguments, and with reason one may do with them whatever one wishes. They

are not flighty. On the contrary, they are reasonable and in no way obstinate…." Even Évreux, usually as sympathetic to the natives as the other Capuchin (Abbeville), hits the same note: "They are great lovers of wine… extremely lecherous… inventors of false news, liars, flighty, inconstant…" Also, see Vasconcelos' *Chronicle of the Society of Jesus*: "They are inconstant, and variable…"

The image of the inconstant savage appears conspicuously in Brazilian historical writing, starting with the founding father of Brazilian historiography— and great reactionary—Varnhagen: "they were false and unfaithful, inconstant and ungrateful…" As is well known, the importation of African labor was frequently justified by invoking the Indians' incapacity to handle work on the sugarcane plantation. Gilberto Freyre's racialist anthropology particularly highlighted the contrast between the animal vigor of the Africans and the vegetal laziness of the Amerindians. But even far more politically-correct authors formulated an Indian/African dichotomy that posited native Brazilian inconstancy as one of the two poles. Thus, S. Buarque de Hollanda:

> [The earlier inhabitants of the land] accommo-
> dated themselves with difficulty… to the careful
> and methodical work demanded by the exploita-
> tion of the sugarcane enterprises. Their sponta-
> neous inclination was towards less sedentary
> activities, which might be carried out without
> any forced regularity, far from the watchful
> eyes and probings of strangers. Versatile in the
> extreme, they found that certain notions of order,
> constancy, and exactitude were inaccessible to
> them—notions that for the European amounted
> to something like a second nature and seemed
> fundamental requirements for the existence of
> civil society.

The motif of the "three races" in the formation of Brazilian nationality tends to involve attributing a predominant talent to each one: for the Indians, perception; for the Africans, emotion; for the Europeans, reason. Indeed, this diagram often becomes a progressive scale, as in Freyre, that evokes the three souls of Aristotelian doctrine. Speaking of Aristotle, patron of the 16th-century debate on the nature and condition of the American natives, I wonder (with all appropriate caveats and fear of ridicule) if he might not have played some role in the history of the vegetal imagery that was applied to Indians. The link would come through the same proverbial inconstancy and indifference to belief. The *Metaphysics* argues that the man who "has no arguments of his own about anything," and in particular who refuses to submit to the principle of non-contradiction, "is really no better than a vegetable." Later on the Philosopher asks a question: if this man "forms no judgment, but 'thinks' and 'thinks not' indifferently, what difference will there be between him and the vegetables?" As is widely known, the man-plant here is the sophist, who, in his radical "relativism," appears as something of an ancestor to the Tupinambá. One might look, finally, at a passage from the *Dialogue on the Conversion of the Heathen*:

> Do you know what is the greatest difficulty I find in them? Being so easy to say yes or *pá* to every-thing, or whatever you like. They approve of everything right away, and with the same ease with which they say *pá* ["yes"], they say *aani* ["no"]...

But no matter how widespread it might be, and no matter how varied the experiences on which it bases itself, the concept of the inconstant nature of the native soul seems to me to derive mainly, in the Brazilian case, from the initial years of missionary proselytism among the Tupian peoples. The problem, the Fathers decided, did not come from the Indians' understanding, which was agile and sharp, but rather from the soul's two other powers: memory and will. These were weak, lax. "It is a people of very weak memory for things of God…" Similarly, the obstacle to be overcome was not the presence of a rival doctrine, but what Vieira described as "the barbarous actions and habits of heathens"—cannibalism and wars of vengeance, drinking sprees, polygyny, nakedness, absence of centralized authority and of stable territorial basis—all that which the first Jesuits labeled, more simply, as "bad habits." Note this passage from Nóbrega, for example, which is probably one of the sources inspiring the conceit of the marble and the myrtle:

> These heathens are not like the heathens surrounding the early Church, who would either quickly mistreat or kill anyone who preached against their idols, or believe in the Gospel, thereby preparing themselves to die for Christ. For since these heathens have no idols for which they die, they believe everything that is said to them. The only difficulty lies in taking away all of their bad habits… which requires extended stay among them… and that we live with them and raise their children, from the time they are small, in doctrine and in good habits…

The Blessed Anchieta, the "Apostle of Brazil," concisely and precisely enumerates the obstacles:

> The impediments that keep the Indians from conversion and perseverance in Christian life are their

inveterate customs... like that of having many wives; their wines, which they drink very regularly, and which ordinarily can be taken away from them only with more difficulty than anything else... Likewise the wars with which they attempt vengeance on enemies, and through which they take new names, and titles of honor; the fact of being naturally but little constant in everything they start, and above all lacking fear and subjection...

Such an image motivated a well-known catechistic strategy. To convert, first civilize; more fruitful than the precarious conversion of adults would be the education of children far from the native environment. Rather than simply preaching the good news, missionaries would incessantly police the civil conduct of the Indians. Assembly, settlement, subjection, education. To inculcate faith, it was necessary first to give the natives law, and king. Conversion depended on an anthropology capable of identifying the *humana impedimenta* ["human obstacles" T.N.] of the Indians, which were of a type that we would today call "sociocultural."

Much has already been written on the cosmological impact caused by the discovery of the New World, on Thomistic Iberian anthropology, on Jesuit proselytism, and on the role of the Society of Jesus in colonial Brazil. I can add nothing to areas beyond my competence. I am interested only in elucidating that thing that the Jesuits and other observers called "inconstancy" among the Tupinambá. It must doubtlessly amount to something real, even if one might like to assign it a different name. If not a mode of *being*, it was a mode of *appearing*, a mode through which missionary eyes saw Tupinambá society. We must situate this mode, more broadly, within the frame of the Indians' ideological bulimia, that intense interest with which they listened to and assimilated the Christian message about God, the soul, and the world. For, I repeat, what exasperated the priests was not any active resistance by the "Brazilians" against the Gospel in the name of another belief, but rather the fact that this people had a perplexing relationship to belief itself. They seemed ready to swallow everything; it was once they appeared to have been won over that they became obstinate, returning to the "vomit of old habits."

Culture as a religious system

The enthusiastic but highly selective acceptance of a
totalizing and exclusive discourse, and the refusal to
follow this discourse to its end, must have seemed
enigmatic to men who devoted themselves to mission,
obedience, and self-denial. Moreover, I think that this
enigma continues to make us uncomfortable as anthropologists, although for different reasons than those that
bothered the old Jesuits. First, savage "inconstancy"
is a theme that still resonates, with its multiple
harmonies, in the ideology of the modern discipli-
narians of the Brazilian Indians. (The anthropology of
the Jesuits, as Menget notes, bore immeasurable fruit
in the legislation and the policies of the Brazilian state
concerning Indians.) Second, and more importantly,
inconstancy in fact corresponds to something that can
be experienced when one lives with many Amerindian
societies. It is something indefinable that marks not
only the psychological tone of people's relationship
to the Western ideological menu, but also—and in a
way much more difficult to analyze—the psychological
tone of people's relationship to themselves, to their
own "authentic" ideas and institutions. Finally, above
all, this indefinable inconstancy constitutes a serious
challenge to current conceptions of culture, whether
anthropological or commonsensical (supposing there
is a difference between the two), and to the connected
themes of acculturation and social change. These
depend profoundly on a paradigm derived from the
notions of belief and conversion.

It helps little to say, as did the Jesuits in their
own way, that the Tupinambá resistance to Christianity

came not from their religion but from their culture. For we, moderns and anthropologists, tend to conceive of culture in a theological mode, as a "system of beliefs" to which individuals adhere, so to speak, religiously. The anthropological reduction of Christianity, such a decisive enterprise for the constitution of our discipline, could not help but impregnate the culture concept with the values of that which it hoped to grasp. "Religion as a cultural system" presupposes an idea of culture as a religious system.

> Naturally, this somewhat ponderous conjecture on the relationship between modern notions of culture and theological notions of belief would demand much work in order to prove helpful. Since Bourdieu, at least, it has become de rigueur to castigate the "theoristic attitude" of anthropologists, which makes them see culture as an architectural system of rules and principles, et cetera. It would be interesting to explore the dependence of this "theoristic" position itself on the theological paradigm. The question of belief, in turn, which continues to haunt the anthropology of the Anglo-Saxon tradition, probably sinks its roots considerably deeper than Hume, directly in the epistemology of the Reformation. As regards the role of the Calvinist doctrine of the symbol in the formation of Victorian religious anthropology (not to mention what it might have contributed towards the—equally Genevan—principle of the arbitrariness of the sign)— that is one more thing that remains to be appropriately elucidated.

We know why the Jesuits chose customs as their main enemy: barbarians of the third class, the Tupinambá did not have a religion properly speaking, only superstitions.

But we moderns do not accept such an ethnocentric distinction. We would say that the missionaries did not see that the "bad habits" of the Tupinambá were their true religion, and that their inconstancy was the result of a deep adherence to a set of beliefs that one has every right to call "religious." The Jesuits, as if they had read their Durkheim but got him somewhat wrong, disastrously separated the sacred and the profane. We, on the other hand, know that custom is not only King and Law, but also God himself. Upon reflection, perhaps the Jesuits also knew this, deep inside; otherwise they would not have quickly identified habits as the great impediment to conversion. Today it is clear that the Tupinambá had a little more than terrible manners. Ever since Métraux, anthropologists have discovered in the testimonies of the first chroniclers a set of myths that hold obvious philosophical significance. Commentators are similarly aware of the importance of shamans and prophets in the religious and political life of these societies. We finally know that the Tupinambá, like the rest of the Tupi-Guarani peoples, possessed a "system of beliefs"—anthropological, theological, cosmological—in which the theme of the "Land without Evil" occupied a major place.

The Tupinambá were, indeed, one of the examples of Acosta's third category of barbarians. Serafim Leite ventures a delicious sophism: since the issue of the conversion of the Brazilian Indians was not *doctrinal* but rather a question of *customs* (his emphasis), there was no violence in the Jesuit proselytism, nor any vileness in the material blackmail that the missionaries practiced against the Indians in order to convert them: "because there is only space for violence when a religion or a rite is torn away, with another being imposed. Now it was not that which occurred." Where irreligion is the cultural system, introducing a religion becomes, shall we say, a merely cultural question. And the stern injunction to *compelle eos intrare* ["make them enter," a theological reference to Luke 14:23 (T.N.)] is re-presented as the solicitous teaching of good manners.

The Jesuits' "mistake" served as a lesson. Today the religious conception of the cultural order enjoys great success inside the progressive Church—but this time in the Indians' favor. Closer than ours to the original values of Christianity, indigenous societies are imagined to sweat religiosity through every pore, to be veritable theodicies in practical form. Thus, replacing the Christological image of incarnation with the anthropological image of "enculturation," the new missionary discovers that it is not the Indians who must be converted, but he himself—since *someone* needs to get converted, after all. Indigenous Culture, appropriately sublimated through a vigorous anagogic interpretation, becomes the quintessence of the good, the beautiful, and the true. Hence the naïve traditionalism of the progressive missionary, hostile to the smallest symptom of anthropophagic *Aufhebung* (in the Oswaldian sense) on the part of his sheep. Hence, too, the missionary's no less naïve belief in his own capacity to transcend his culture of origin and become miraculously enculturated by the other. The old Jesuits, at least, knew that the business of leaving behind bad habits was as a rule very complicated.

(Oswald de Andrade (1890-1954), poet and pioneer of Brazilian modernism, penned the famous *Manifesto Antropófago* in 1928. He argued that colonists had not consumed native Brazilians; on the contrary, native Brazilians had eaten the culture of the colonists, seizing what they respected and ingesting it in order to produce an even stronger synthesis. Andrade's account can be read in terms of Hegel's notion of *Aufhebung*, the apparently contradictory "sublation" or dialectical process in which a concept gets both changed and preserved by being synthesized with another concept. Incidentally, Andrade wrote the *Manifesto* explicitly "against Father Vieira." (T.N.)).

So "they" had a religion. But this only makes the problem more difficult to solve: "they say that they want to be like us...;" "they wish to be Christians like us..." Why, after all, would the savages wish to be like us? If they possessed a religion, and if anyway a culture is a system of beliefs, then one might be forgiven for wondering what kind of religion and what kind of system this was, a religion and a system that contained inside themselves the wish for their own destruction. Looking at inconstancy the other way around, one must ask why the Tupinambá were inconstant in relation to their own culture-religion. Why, despite what Vieira said about the difficulty of making them deaf to the "fancies of their ancestors," did they seem so ready to lend such an eager ear to foreign fibs?

They also might, however, mock the Catholic doctrine, especially after they had had time to experience the injustice of the White men. Vieira, scandalized, tells of the state in which he found the mission to the Tobajaras of the Ibiapaba Mountains in the middle of the 17th century. "In the veneration of temples, of images, of crosses, and of sacraments many of them were as Calvinist and Lutheran as if they had been born in England or Germany. They call the Church 'church of Moanga,' which means false church, and the Christian doctrine 'moranduba of the abarés,' which means lies of the priests...". But well before this, Hans Staden had already confronted indigenous sarcasm in the face of European religion: "I had to sing something for them, and I chanted religious songs, which I had to explain to them in their language. I said, 'I sang about my God.' They replied that my God was a piece of filth, in their language, *teõuira*..." I suspect that this word is the same as Léry's *tyvire*, which means passive sodomite.

In the 16th century, the religion of the Tupinambá—with no rites, no idols, and no priests— amounted to an enigma in the eyes of the Jesuits. Instead, the Jesuits saw "culture" as the hard core of the elusive indigenous being. Today, the problem seems to be how to explain why such a culture would, in the first place, welcome so benevolently the theology and cosmology of the invaders, as if these alien constructs (and the aliens themselves) had been prefigured in some cranny of the Amerindian cultural mechanism. It was as if the unheard-of belonged to tradition, as if the unseen were already stored in memory. A demonstration effect produced by the recognition of the technological superiority of the strangers? A fortuitous coincidence between the contents of the native mythology and some aspects of the invading society? Such hypotheses contain a kernel of truth, but, rather than explaining something, they themselves must be explained. For they suppose a more fundamental orientation, an "*opening to the Other*" characteristic of Amerindian thought. In the Tupinambá case this was particularly extensive and intensive. There, the other was not merely good to think—the other was necessary for thinking.

Thus the problem is to determine the meaning of this mix of versatility and obstinacy, docility and recalcitrance, enthusiasm and indifference with which the Tupinambá received the Good News. It is to see beyond the apparent "weak memory" and the "deficiency of will" of the Indians, their faithless belief. It is, finally, to understand the object of that obscure desire to be the other but—herein lies the mystery—on one's own terms.

Our current idea of "culture" projects an anthropological landscape peopled by marble statues, not ones made of myrtle: a classical museum rather than a baroque garden. We think that every society tends to persevere in its own being, and that culture is the reflexive form of that being; we believe that a violent, massive pressure is needed for it to deform and transform. But, above all, we believe that the being of a society is its perseverance: memory and tradition are the identitarian marble out of which culture is made. Moreover, we judge that, once they have been converted into something other than themselves, societies that have lost their tradition have no way back. There is no returning; the previous form has been defaced for good. The most that can be hoped for is an exhibition made of simulacra and false memories, where "ethnicity" and bad conscience feed on the remains of the extinct culture.

But perhaps, for societies whose foundation (or lack thereof) is the relationship to others, and not self-identity, none of this makes the least sense. In the words of James Clifford:

> Stories of cultural contact and change have been structured by a pervasive dichotomy: absorption by

the other *or* resistance to the other [...] Yet what if identity is conceived not as a boundary to be maintained but as a nexus of relations and transactions actively engaging a subject? The story or stories of interaction must then be more complex, less linear and theological. What changes when the subject of "history" is no longer Western? How do stories of contact, resistance, and assimilation appear from the standpoint of groups in which exchange rather than identity is the fundamental value to be sustained?

Of Hell and Glory

Before appearing as Vieira's ephemeral and imprecise myrtle statues, the Tupinambá were seen as men of wax, ready for the impression of a mold. Nóbrega's first letter was optimistic:

> All those who talk to us say that they want to be like us, only that they have no way of covering themselves like us, and this is the only obstacle. If they hear the sound of the Mass, they awaken right away, and whatever they see us do, they do in its entirety: they kneel, they beat their chests, they lift their hands to the sky; and one of their leaders is learning to read and takes lessons each day with great care, and in two days knew the full ABC, and we taught him the sign of the cross, taking all with much desire. He says that he wants to be a Christian and not eat human flesh, nor have more than one woman and other things; only that he must go to war and, taking captives, sell them and use them for himself, because those of this land are always at war with others and thus they all live in discord. They eat one another, that is, their opponents. These are people who have no knowledge of God, nor idols, and they do everything that one tells them.

Here are some of the crucial elements of the problem: mimetic enthusiasm for the ritual apparatus of the missionaries; willingness to leave behind bad habits; a religious vacuum begging to be filled. The Tupinambá appear alienated, slaves of a pathetic desire for recognition. Discreetly, of course, the text refers to a small intransigence of that very solicitous leader: he gives up cannibalism and other terrible customs, but he will continue to go to war. This intransigence shows up again in an anecdote of Thevet's, where he sketches out an additional facet of the "encounter" between the Tupi and the missionaries:

Also a king of this country, named Pinda-houssoub, whom I went to see while he was in bed, stricken with a continuous fever, asked me what happened to souls after they left the body: and—since I responded to him that they went with Toupan, up there in the sky, with those who had lived well, and who had not taken vengeance on their enemies for injury—he, believing me, entered into a great contemplation. [...] [T]wo days later he sent for me, and when I was in front of him said to me, So, I have heard you tell great stories about a Toupan, who can do anything: I beg you, speak with him on my behalf, and make him heal me, and then I will stand, and in health I will make great gifts to you, and I want to be all dressed up like you, and even have a great beard, and honor Toupan as you honor him. To which I made answer, that if he wanted to heal, and believe in the one who made the sky, the earth, and the sea, and if he no longer believed [...] in their Karaibas and sorcerers, and if he did not take revenge, nor eat his enemies, as he had done for all of his life [...] doubtlessly he would be healed, and his soul after his death would not be tormented by cruel spirits, as those of his fathers and mothers were. To which this master Kinglet responded to me that being healed by the power of Toupan he would willingly agree to all of the terms I had set forth for him, excepting one, which was to not have vengeance on his enemies: and even when Toupan commanded him to not do it, he would not know how to agree: Or if by some accident he did agree, he would deserve to die of shame.

Pindabuçu's question about the posthumous fate of souls becomes even more intriguing when we see that it appears, in the text of the *Cosmographie*, after an exposition of Tupinambá personal eschatology, which precisely revolved around warrior prowess and vengeance, destining the brave to paradise and cowards to a miserable existence on Earth. It is to be noted that the indigenous "kinglet" did not argue with Thevet in metaphysical terms—refusing Christian blackmail in favor of a different soteriology—but rather in ethical ones, with the simple affirmation of a categorical imperative. We may note, finally, that for him, as for Nóbrega's leader, vengeance is the non-negotiable point, not the cannibalism associated with it.

We will return to the problem of cannibalism and war; for now, let us stay with the request that Pindabuçu made for information on the Beyond. It was probably this type of inquiry that delighted the Jesuits, certain of having found the ideal customers for their merchandise. Thus, rejoiced Nóbrega, "they do not have certainty of any god and whatever you tell them about they believe..." Asking for more missionaries from Portugal, he specified that these did not need to be erudite: "Here a few letters is enough, because everything is blank paper and all one must do is write as one pleases..." Pero Correia tells of the leaders' desire to learn the faith of Christ, and Leonardo Nunes proffers a possible explanation for this desire:

And in regards to the heathens of the land, I see so many signs that, because of the great preparedness I see, they often place me in doubt as to whether I should leave the Christians altogether and present myself to them along with all of the Brothers, following the wishes of these heathens, that we walk amongst them, because of the great will they show [...] And because we have not yet gone to teach them many souls have been lost, because their desires are great to meet God and to know what they have to do to save themselves, because they greatly fear death and the day of judgment and Hell, of which they have already had some news, after our Lord led the most dear Pedro Correa to be our Brother, because in the talks he has with them I always tell him to mention it, so that fear may place them in very great perturbation of mind.

The news of the Final Judgment caused great marveling. And the requests to the priests for long life and health were constant: "Their plan is for us to give them much life and health and support without work, as their sorcerers promise them;" "because they think that we can give them health..." In the account of Anchieta's delegation to the Tamoios, the missionary recalled the speech he gave on arrival; he said that he had come so that God

might give them an abundance of provisions, health, and victory over their enemies and other similar things, without ascending any higher, because this nation, without such a staircase, does not want to climb to heaven...

The leader of the village listened with wonder to the discussion of "Hell and glory," and warned his companions not to harm the missionary: "If we ourselves fear our sorcerers, how much more fear should we have for the priests, who must be true saints..." He then asked for Anchieta's intercession with God: "pray to him that he give me long life, so that I can align myself with you against my own..."

Although the Jesuits were the ideal recipients, this request for long life seems to also have been directed to other eminent Europeans. See Thevet on the appeals to Villegagnon: "make it so that we do not die at all..." (It is true that this request was made in the context of an epidemic that was decimating the Indians, who suspected French witchcraft. Thus the request of "no death" made to the commander of Fort Coligny implies a conception of him as the chief sorcerer, not as the purely positive dispenser of long life. One should recall that the Tupinambá *pajé* and *karaiba* frequently threatened the Indians with magical death, according to the chroniclers.) It did not take long, however, for the attribution of wonder-working powers to the missionaries to turn into the reverse. Baptismal water, a powerful pathogenic vector (and moreover frequently administered in extremis) was quickly associated with death, and rejected with horror by the Indians, who came to flee the arrival of priests, and to hand war captives over to them out of fear of sorcery. Furthermore, it was believed that baptismal water ruined the meat of prisoners, making this meat poisonous to those who ate it—which may not have been far from the truth. The eschatological message of the priests came to be heard as an evil omen:

(from Lourenço): [Since] I saw them together I said to an interpreter who was headed in that direction that he tell them something about God, and they all listened, but since he came to speak about death they did not want to hear it, and they told the interpreter to not speak any more...

(from Grã:) [T]he fact of speaking about death close by them is very odious, because it is their conviction that this brings it on them, and this thought is enough for them to die in their imaginations; and many times they have begged me that I not bring it on them...

The great popularizers of this theory of the lethality of baptism were the *pajé* (shaman healers) and the *karaiba* (shaman-prophets).

Division in Paradise

Long life, abundance, victory in war: the themes of the "Land without Evil." The priests of the Society of Jesus were assimilated to the Tupinambá *karaiba*. This must be seen in the context of the classification of Europeans as supernaturally-powerful figures: *Mair* (or "Maíra"), the name of an important demiurge, was the ethnonym for the French; and *karaiba* (a term applied to demiurges and culture heroes, gifted with high shamanic science) came to designate Europeans in general, not only the priests. Speaking of the *karaiba* and their practices, Anchieta clarifies:

> All of this nonsense is called by a general word, Caraiba, which means something like a holy thing, or supernatural; and for this reason they gave this name to the Portuguese, as soon as they came, seeing them as a great entity, as something from another world, since they had come so far on top of the waters.

Thevet suggests more directly that the assimilation of the Europeans to the mythical *karaiba* was already pre-formed in Tupinambá religion. The clever friar seems to have been the first to perceive the generality of the Amerindian association between the arrival of White people and the return of mythical heroes or divine figures:

> I will spend no other time on the argument about whether the devil knows and is familiar with future things... But one case I will surely tell you, that a long time before we arrived there the spirit had predicted to them our coming: and I know it, not

only from them themselves, but also from several Portuguese Christians, who were kept as prisoners of this barbarous people: And so much was said to the first Spaniards who discovered Peru, and Mexico.

There are, in fact, strong indications that the "reading" of the Whites in terms of *Mair* and *karaiba* was more than an inoffensive metaphor, and that the technological skill of the invaders played a role in this assimilation. Here one can begin to perceive the tip of a mythological iceberg, which may help one to make sense of the requests to priests and other eminent Europeans for long life. Tupian myths about the separation between humans and culture heroes or demi-urges are also myths on the origin of mortality; these myths hearken back, in several ways, to the "origin of short life" theme analyzed by Lévi-Strauss. It was this same mythical matrix involving the separation between humans and culture heroes—foundation of the human condition, that is, the social and mortal condition—that proved useful for thinking the Indian/European difference. The myths on the origin of the White man, among the Tupi as with many other Amerindians, use the motif of the *wrong choice*, characteristic of the short-life complex, to explain the material superiority of the Whites. It thus seemed imaginable that, having made the "right choice" at the beginning of time, Whites also possessed the divine science of non-mortality, the attribute of the *Mair* and the *karaiba*, whose "*successeurs et vrays enfans*" ["successors and true children"] they were.

For Thevet, the French were taken as children of Maire Monan because of their great technological talents, and because they were masters of many things never before seen. The problem is that the Portuguese, who must not have been very different from the French in this regard, were never called by the ethnonym *Mair*, but rather *Peró*, a name probably derived from the personal name Pero or Pedro. Anchieta believed that the use of the term *Mair* for the French came from the fact that this mythological character was the enemy of Sumé, a figure who, to some degree, would be associated with the Portuguese. (I believe it must have been Anchieta himself who, relating Sumé to Saint Thomas, linked his fellow countrymen with the figure.) Another possible reason for the French to have been "mairized" may lie in the skin color of the Norman sailors, lighter than that of the Portuguese, and their blond hair. (An alternative name for the French was *ajuru-juba*, "yellow parrots.") The theme of the Maíra's very white skin appears in some Tupian myths, being associated with the motif of immortality attained by changing skin.

The general Tupinambá term for the Europeans seems to have been *karaiba* itself, and Anchieta's explanation is a reasonable one. The etymology of this word, widespread among contemporary Tupi as an ethnic name for Whites, is uncertain. Montoya argued that the Guarani form *caraíba* connects with the lexeme *cara*, which (according to him) means "talented, clever, astute." And then there is the thorny problem of figuring out whether or not the word *karaiba* has anything to do with Caribs, the Caribbean, et cetera. In the Upper Xingu, *karaiba* is the term used by all tribes for Whites. Von den Steinen felt convinced that this was a term of Carib origin. It is worth pointing out that the Europeans, called karaiba, and initially treated as such personages, ended up bringing the Indians the exact opposite of that which the karaiba promised:

instead of migratory wandering, forced settlement;
instead of long life and abundance without effort, death
from epidemics and slave labor; instead of victory over
enemies, prohibitions on war and cannibalism; instead
of matrimonial freedom, new restrictions.

Not Thevet, but rather Abbeville, directly presents us
with the theme of the "wrong choice" as origin of the
cultural differences between Indians and Whites, in
the form of a choice (offered to humans by god(s))
between indigenous and European arms. This pattern
is widespread elsewhere as well. It is found again,
for example, in the Upper Xingu and Northwest
Amazonian mythologies. In the latter, in both the
Barasana and the Maku versions, one can find the
"Jacob and Esau" motif involving the inversion in the
order of seniority between a pair of (twin) brothers,
which Abbeville also detects in Tupinambá myth.
(Note that the Maku account concerns the Maku/
Tukano difference.)

R. DaMatta, in pioneering works, demonstrated
the structural relationship between Timbira myths on
the origin of culture (specifically, culinary fire) and the
arrival of Whites. More recently, Lévi-Strauss observed
that the Auké narrative analyzed by DaMatta is an
inversion of the Tupinambá myth on the origin of White
people, a myth collected by Thevet as one episode of
a vast cosmogonic cycle. For my part, I would suggest
a relationship between the myths on the genesis of
Whites, on the one hand, and the etiology of short life
or of mortality on the other, the relevance of the latter
to the origin-of-fire-and-culture complex having been
explicated in *The Raw and the Cooked*. Lévi-Strauss
approaches the myths of short life in terms of a "code
of the five senses." One could see the motif of the
"wrong choice" as a modulation of this code: instead
of mistakes related to sensibility (in the Kantian sense),

we would here have an error connected to the lack of "good sense" (or understanding.) The divorce between the Tupinambá demiurges and humans, fruit of the ungratefulness or aggression of the latter, can similarly figure as the prime example of a wrong choice, an absence of discernment on the part of humans (i.e. of Indians, since it was through them that the rupture produced the White/Indian difference.)

The Northwest Amazonian narrative analyzed by Hugh-Jones is a variant quite close to the Tupinambá myth. Space does not here permit a detailed analysis of the relationship between them; let me only call attention to one aspect of the Northwest Amazonian myth. It establishes a direct connection between the origin of short life (for the Indians) and the origin of Whites; the latter are similar to spiders, snakes, and women in their capacity for long life (menstruation here being conceived as a "change of skin.") White people change a cultural skin, clothing; thus, technical knowledge connects with immortality. The theme of the change of skin as a sign or instrument of immortality is central in the cosmology of various contemporary Tupian groups; among the Araweté it is associated with the *Maï* (cf. the Tupinambá *Mair*).

We should also mention a negative transformation of the theme, one which draws a causal association between the immortality of Whites and the short life of the Indians: the famous Andean and sub-Andean *pishtaco* or *pelacara* figure, a monstrous hypostasis of the Whites that hunts Indians in order to take the skin off of their faces (or the fat off of their bodies) and use it for the rejuvenation of their own people. The Piro studied by Gow claimed that the *pelacara* supplied plastic surgeons in the large cities, thus constructing a brilliant modern reading of the motif of skin-changing.

Let us clearly state that this does not mean that any "cult" was devoted to the Europeans. As soon as they showed their nastier side, they were killed like any other enemy; moreover, their cowardice before the executioner's mace provoked amazement and mockery. The Tupi-Guarani religion, as Hélène Clastres has shown, was based on the idea that the separation between the human and the divine was not an unbridgeable ontological barrier, but something to be overcome. Humans and gods were consubstantial and commensurable; humanity was a condition, not a nature. Such a theology, a stranger to transcendence, was as ill-suited for bad conscience as it was unfitted to an attitude of humility. But neither did the theology incline towards the "dialectical" inverses of these sentiments. The Tupi could not conceive of the arrogance of a chosen people, or the compulsion to reduce the other to one's own image. If the Europeans desired the Indians because they saw in them either useful animals or potential Europeans and Christians, the Tupi desired the Europeans in their full alterity. The Europeans offered to the Tupi an opportunity for self-transfiguration, a sign of the reunion of that which had been rent asunder at the origin of culture, and they were therefore capable of expanding the human condition, or even going beyond it. Thus it was perhaps the Amerindians, not the Europeans, who saw the "vision of paradise" in the American (mis)(sed)encounter. The Indians had no maniac desire to impose their identity on the other, nor did they reject the other in favor of their own ethnic excellence. Rather, they aimed, by producing a relationship with the other—a relationship that had always existed, in a virtual mode—to transform their own identity. The inconstancy of the savage soul, in its moment of openness, is the expression of a mode of being where "exchange rather than identity is the fundamental value to be sustained," to recall Clifford's profound formulation.

So relational affinity, not substantial identity, was the value to be affirmed. Let us recall that the "theology" of some Tupian peoples gets formulated quite directly in the terms of a sociology of exchange: the difference between gods and humans is explained in the language of a marriage alliance, the same language that the Tupinambá employed to think about and incorporate their enemies. The Europeans came to share a space already populated with the Tupian figures of alterity: gods, affines, and enemies, whose attributes bled into each other. From this standpoint one can make sense of the various commentaries on the "great honor" sought by the Indians when they gave their daughters and sisters in marriage to Europeans. Beyond the calculations of economic benefit—having sons- or brothers-in-law among the lords of so many goods was certainly a powerful motive—one must also take into consideration the non-material dimension, since one is speaking of "honor." It was in terms of this same idea of honor that the chroniclers interpreted the granting of women to war captives, before their ceremonial execution. It seems to me that "honor" here serves as a placeholder for the primordial value of Tupinambá culture: the capture of alterities outside the *socius* and their subordination to the "internal" social logic, through the prototypical apparatus of matrimonial indebtedness. These were the central motor and main motif of the society, responsible for its centrifugal tendency. Mortal war to enemies and enthusiastic hospitality to Europeans, cannibal vengeance and ideological voracity—all expressed the same propensity and the same desire: to absorb the other and, in the process, to change oneself. (Therefore it was as much the case that the Tupinambá "wanted to turn White" as it was that they wanted the Whites to turn Tupinambá. The Jesuit letters abound with complaints about bad Christians going native, entering into polygamous marriages with Indian women, killing enemies in the central square, taking ceremonial names, and even eating people.) Gods, enemies, and Europeans were figures of potential affinity, different transforms of an alterity that attracted and that needed to be attracted— an alterity without which the world would sink into indifference and paralysis.

Questions like the one that Pindabuçu asked Thevet resound in the missionary literature. The Jesuits' eschatological preaching had great success, at least at the beginning. It linked up with a key question of the indigenous religion, the refusal of personal mortality. Moreover, the Christian apocalyptic message coincided with the native theme of the cosmic catastrophe that would destroy the earth. But it seems to me that such coinciding Christian themes—obviously filtered out of a larger set of concepts that was in other regards utterly foreign to native ideas—were not the only factor driving the special attention that the Tupinambá lavished upon the priests' news of the Beyond. To the very extent that they came "from another world" (in Anchieta's formulation), the Europeans were messengers of exteriority, familiars with souls and with death. Like the *karaiba* or "holy ones" to whom they were assimilated, their province was non-presence; like indigenous magicians, the Europeans were in the proper speaking position to talk about that which was beyond the domain of experience.

Concerning apocalyptic motives: beyond the contemporary Guarani, whose typical case is the Apapocuva of Nimuendaju, see also the Wayãpi and the Araweté. Hélène Clastres argues that practically no mention of the indigenous theme of the apocalypse can be found in the chronicles (except a very vague passage of Thevet's). In the *Letters of the First Jesuits of Brazil*, however, Anchieta tells an anecdote about an old Indian man whom he taught: "What made the greatest impression on him was the mystery of the Resurrection, which he repeated many times, saying, 'The true God is Jesus who left the tomb and went to Heaven and must later come back, very full of ire, to burn all things.'" It is obvious that one can see here the influence of the Last Judgment, but I also suspect the presence of the universal conflagration of Tupian mythology. At any rate, it was this Christian theme that struck the old man.

I do not think we can take as final explanation the undeniable convergence in contents between Tupi-Guarani religion and the missionaries' word. Requests just as disturbing (to anthropologists and other culturalists) as those of the Tupinambá can still be observed today: P. Gow tells how the Piro, whose cosmology does not particularly resemble that of the sixteenth-century Tupi, asked the same type of question to the missionaries of the Summer Institute of Linguistics, delegating to them and to other *gringos* the cognitive competence—a competence hardly free from ambiguity—to know about that which happened on the Outside: death, the limits of the inhabited world, the skies. Many other observers testify to analogous facts. For this reason, I have reservations about H. Clastres' hypothesis that the Jesuits' success among the Guarani (let us note in passing that they had much less success among the coastal Tupi) occurred because of the analogies between Christian eschatology and the theme of the Land Without Evil—with the added benefit, for the Christians, that their vision did not run the risk of disproof, since, unlike things promised in native prophetic discourse, the Christian paradise could not be reached while alive. It seems to me that one must seek to explain the (inconstant) receptivity to European discourse not only, or principally, on the level of ideological contents. Rather, the explanation must take place along two lines: on the one hand, at the level of socially-determined forms of (self-)relationship to culture or tradition; on the other hand, at the level of the (cultural) structures of ontological presupposition. A culture is not a system of beliefs, but rather —since it must be something—a set of potential structurations of experience, capable of supporting varying "traditional" contents and of absorbing new ones. It is a "culturating" apparatus, or one constitutive of the processing of beliefs. Even on the constituted plane of culturated culture, I think it is more interesting to inquire into the conditions that allow certain cultures to give foreign "beliefs" a status of supplementarity or alternativity in relation to their own "beliefs."

The missionaries, in particular, were taken to be similar to the *karaiba*, and knew how to make use of this. From the beginning, their wandering nature and their hortatory discourse made them resemble the *karaiba*. They also came to adopt morning preaching, in the style of the shamans and the chiefs. They liberally employed song as an instrument of seduction, taking advantage of the high reputation enjoyed by music and good singers (including the *karaiba*) among the Tupinambá. They probably benefited from the same immunity that protected the wandering prophets and other "masters of speech." They even met, with appropriate mental reservations, certain native demands, promising victory over enemies and material abundance. To requests for cures and long life, they responded with baptism and preaching about eternal life. And they accepted, slightly concerned, even imputations of the power to tell the future.

Of course, the Tupinambá also knew how to take advantage of the missionaries. First of all, if the *karaiba* proved, on many occasions, inflexible opponents of the priests, nonetheless more than a few of the *karaiba* appropriated the Christian discourse, whether by way of challenge or opportunistically:

> (from Nóbrega:) I took pains to meet with a sorcerer, the greatest one of this land. [...] I asked him *in qua potestate hec faciebat* [through what authority he did this], if he had communications with God who made the sky and the earth and reigned in Heaven [...] He responded with little shame, that he was a god and had been born a god, and he presented to me there a person to whom he said he had given health, and that the God of the skies was his friend, and appeared to him in clouds, and in thunder, and in lightning...

Another "wandering sorcerer," from a village in Pernambuco,

> (from Rodrigues:) seeing the trust that the Fathers enjoyed among the people, said that he was their relative and that the Fathers told the truth, and that he had already died and passed from this life and came back to life as the aforementioned Fathers said,

and that they should therefore believe in him, and give him in the meantime their daughters upon his request...

Secondly, the innumerable epistolary references to leaders desirous of conversion suggest that politically powerful men, household heads or village chiefs, avidly seized the opportunity to possess a religious knowledge alternative to that of the karaiba. We do not, however, need to accept in its entirety the hypothesis of H. Clastres about the "contradiction between the political and the religious" in precolonial Tupian society. We can instead see here a dispute between competing eminences. The use of the priests for the attainment of one's own political objectives, moreover, was common: the Tamoio of Iperoig received Anchieta's delegation in order to win the Portuguese as allies against their traditional adversaries, the Tupinquim of São Vicente. Apparently little inclined to any segmentary opposition, the Tupi sold their "souls" to the Europeans in order to keep up their bodily war against other Tupi. This helps us understand why the Indians would not compromise on the imperative of vengeance. For them religion, their own or that of others, was subordinate to bellicose ends: instead of having wars of religion, like those that blossomed in Europe that century, they practiced a religion of war.

On the Hardness of Belief

The priests were, then, seen as a particularly strong type of *karaiba*. But here we come face to face with the great problem: did the Tupinambá believe in their prophets? The first Jesuit letters lament— although not without anticipating the benefits—the credulity of the Indians, who allowed themselves to be led blindly by the holy ones: "whichever one among them wants to make himself their god, that one they believe, and place full trust in him..."; "there are among them some whom they fear as being holy and they trust these so much that whatever these order them to do, they do it." Well-known shamanic practices include the ceremonies carried out by the shamans for the transfusion of spiritual powers; the cures, premonitions, and supernatural deeds they were trusted to carry out; their mediating functions between the world of the living and of the dead—not to speak of the formidable migrations unleashed and led by the *karaiba* in search of the Land Without Evil. There is, in sum, no doubt that shamans and prophets benefited from "immense prestige" among the Tupinambá, playing a key religious role. What remains to be seen is whether such prestige, which was in large part transferred onto the Christian missionaries, can be translated into the politico-theological language of faith and belief.

Although the Jesuits testify to the harmful prestige of the *karaiba*, it is strange that the *karaiba* do not figure in the letters as the main, or even a major, obstacle to the conversion of the heathen, but rather as a supplementary problem, part of the complex of native bad habits, and incapable, in themselves, of hampering the desire for Christianization.

> (from Nóbrega:) The heathen, who seem to take as their beatitudes the killing of their adversaries and the eating of human flesh, and the keeping of many wives, are much improving, and all of our work consists in keeping them away from that. Because the rest is easy, since they do not have idols, although there are among them some who make themselves into holy ones and promise them health and victory over their enemies. With all of the heathen to whom I have spoken on this coast, among none have I found repugnance for what I was saying: all want and desire to be Christians, but leaving their habits seems rough to them...

> (from Blázquez:) [T]aking away from them the killings and the eating of human flesh, and removing from them the sorcerers and making them live with only one woman...

During the period of Jesuit disappointment that quickly followed the initial optimism, the typical savage inconstancy outweighed in importance the actions of the native "holy ones" as an obstacle to conversion: "because since they do not have anyone to worship, except a holy one who comes once a year, [...] they easily say that they want to be Christians, and just as easily turn back..." Little by little, the priests began to perceive that the type of belief devoted to the *karaiba* was not exactly that which they would like transferred to themselves and to their doctrine. "Concerning some of those who make themselves into holy ones amongst them, they trust sometimes and sometimes not, because most of the time they catch the holy ones in lies." This Jesuit criticism should not be chalked up to mere spite or professional jealousy. The skepticism, the priests realized, extended to themselves:

> (from Nóbrega:) And it is worth little to go preach to them and then return home, because, although they trust somewhat, it is not enough to uproot them from their old habits, and they believe in us as they believe in their sorcerers, who sometimes lie to them and sometimes manage to speak truth...

Prophets who fell into disgrace among their followers were frequently killed. In some cases, like that of the sorcerer of Pernambuco reported by Vicente Rodrigues (see above), it was the priests themselves who were responsible for this disbelief. Doubtlessly, a worrisome situation: it would not be this type of conditional attachment to the truth of prophesies and the efficacy of cures that would predispose one to revealed religion. The Tupinambá style of religiosity did not serve as the proper model for creating an environment for authentic faith: "although there is no idolatry in this land, but rather certain holy ones whom they say that they neither believe nor refuse to believe..." They neither believe nor refuse to believe: the Indians, it seems, could manage to believe neither in God, nor in the principle of the excluded middle. Or, as Vieira would later say, "even after they have come to believe, they are unbelieving." The missionaries, who a few years earlier had insisted on the universal credulity of the heathens, realized that things were far more complicated, and that the belief in the holy ones and in the fancies of the ancestors did not trace out the negative space of a conversion.

This Tupinambá version of the *"problème de l'incroyance au seizième siècle,"* to evoke the celebrated book of Lucien Febvre, presents us with two linked aspects: one cognitive and the other political. When Vieira said that the gardener of his myrtle statues had to cut "that which blooms in their eyes, so that they may believe what they do not see," perhaps he was making more than an allusion to the Gospel. Similarly, when the chroniclers depict the Tupinambá modifying certain cosmological declarations with particular phrases—"according to what our *karaiba* tells us," "the place that our *pajé* say they have seen"—this may mean more (or, rather, less) than the recognition of the absolute authority of the shamans and the prophets in matters of the Beyond.

The Tupinambá language, as is common in Amerindian cultures, distinguishes between the narration of events personally experienced by the speaker and the narration of those heard from third parties. My experience with the Araweté, a Tupian people that possesses many affinities with the Tupinambá—including the centrality of the figure of the shamans as creators and spreaders of cosmological knowledge— inclines me to take declarations like "so say our *pajé*" as citational formulas that mark the speaker's non-experiential relationship to the topic of the discourse. In the case of the Araweté, where shamans proliferate as do accounts of what happens in Heaven with the dead and the gods, all of this is clearly associated with a distinction between knowledge obtained by one's own senses and knowledge obtained through the (direct or indirect) experience of others. The two kinds of knowledge do not possess the same epistemic status.

I am far from thinking that the Araweté "do not believe what they do not see;" but they take great care to distinguish what they have seen from what they have heard, and this distinction is especially marked in the case of cosmological information that they give or request. I do not doubt that they believe in their shamans, but in a way that Vieira would probably describe with the phrase, "even after they have come to believe, they are unbelieving." For it certainly has no similarity to a revealed truth, and the notion of dogma is completely foreign to them. It is quite clear that the varied shamanic creations converge on a virtual focal-point that has all of the characteristics of a system; but I do not think that it is a system of "beliefs." Indeed, the proliferation of shamans and shamanistic discourses prevents the solidification of any orthodoxy. Where there are no true believers, there can be no heretics. Would the Tupinambá case have been any different?

The epistemic problem was in fact political, as the Jesuits perceived:

(from Correia:) [I]t seems to me that one must devote much work to them, and one of the reasons, indeed one of the most important, is that they do not have a king, but rather in each Town and house there is a Leader. Thus it is necessary to go from hamlet to hamlet. [...] And if there were a king, once he were converted, all would be...

(from Anchieta:) They are not subject to any king or chief and they only hold in some esteem those who did some deed worthy of a strong man. For this reason, often when we judge them won over,

they become recalcitrant, because there is no-one to
oblige them to obey by force...

But it is in the *Dialogue of the Conversion of the Heathen*
that the nail is hit on the head:

> If they had a king, they could be converted, or if
> they worshipped something; but, since they do not
> even know what believing or worshipping is, they
> cannot understand the preaching of the Gospel,
> because it is based on making people believe in and
> worship only one God, and serve Him alone; and
> since these heathens do not even worship anything,
> everything one tells them turns into nothing.

Here it is: the savages believe in nothing
because they worship nothing. And they worship
nothing, at the end of the day, because they obey
no-one. The absence of centralized power did not
only make conversion logistically difficult (with no
cujus regio principle in effect, the missionaries had to
vend retail rather than wholesale); it made conversion,
above all, logically difficult. The people of Brazil could
not worship and serve a sovereign God because they
did not have sovereigns, nor did they serve anyone.
Their inconstancy flowed, thus, from the absence of
subjection: "there is no-one to oblige them to obey by
force..." To believe is to obey, Paul Veyne reminds us; it
is to yield to revealed truth, to worship the source from
which it emanates, to venerate its representatives. In
the Tupinambá mode of belief there was no space for a
total surrender to a foreign word: "since [they] have no
idols for which they die," they could not have religion
and faith, both of which require the disposition to die
for something. Mode of believing, mode of being. Luís

de Grã concludes philosophically: "and that which it seemed would help them to be Christians, namely, not having idols, it seems that this very thing hinders them, because they do not have any sense." Inconstancy, indifference, nothingness: "What I take as the greatest obstacle for the people of all of these nations is their own condition, that they do not feel anything strongly, neither spiritual loss nor temporal, there is nothing for which they have a very sensitive sentiment, nor one that lasts them long..."

The validation of the native cosmology through recourse to the word of the pajé and the prophets did not mean, therefore, a "belief" in this word, in the politico-theological sense of the term, because what was missing was precisely the aspect of subjection, of abdication of judgment and of will. The Protestant Léry noted with a certain perverse pleasure:

> Furthermore, our Toüoupinambaoults [...] despite all of the ceremonies that they perform, do not worship by bending the knees or according to other exterior signs. They worship neither their Caraïbes nor their Maracas, nor any creature whatsoever.

Léry's reference to the *maracá* is interesting, because the Jesuits' insistence on the fact that the savages lacked idols did not mean that they practiced a religion without any kind of material objectification. The shamanistic rattles, on top of possessing an evident magic and symbolic importance, received anthropomorphic decoration, and spoke with their owners; and there are scattered references to drawings and objects supposed to represent spirits. (Less theological minds, like that of Hans Staden, took the rattles themselves as objects of belief: "the savages believe in a thing that grows like a gourd.") Similarly, the Jesuits and other chroniclers write profusely about the signs of respect granted to the wandering *karaiba*: the cleaning of the paths that led them to the villages, the welcoming hymns, the gifts of food, the rights of extraterritoriality. The authors also mention the fear that these shaman-prophets inspired, with their capacity to cast death upon those who displeased them. Naturally, the chroniclers felt scandalized when they heard the *karaiba* describe themselves as "gods and children of gods," born of virgins, et cetera. However, none of this sufficed to make up, in European eyes, a religion and a rite, given the absence of the indispensable "fear and subjection" (Anchieta); the Tupinambá did not *worship* these objects and people, since they did not know how to feel properly religious reverence and fear, the true foundations of a belief worthy of the name.

Thus we see that the three "constitutive absences" of the Brazilian peoples maintained a causal link with each other: the Indians did not have faith because they did not have law, and they did not have law because they did not have a king. Their language had neither the sounds (Fs, Ls, and Rs; see above) nor the meanings. True belief supposes regular submission to rule, and this in turn supposes the exercise of coercion by a sovereign. Because they did not have a king, they believed the priests; for the same (un)reason—because they did not have a king—they failed to believe. Their refusal of the State, to recall a famous theme, thus did not manifest itself only, or principally, in a prophetic discourse that denied social order. This refusal already lived embedded in the people's relationship to all *discourse*, that is, to an order of reasons with totalizing pretension, and this included the word of the *karaiba*. The Tupinambá did everything the prophets and priests told them to do—except what they didn't want to do.

Let me caution that I do not see the Tupinambá as a group of skeptical empiricists; nor do I think that, by suggesting that it is inadequate to equate a culture to a system of beliefs, I necessarily open the door to the utilitarianism of practical reason (in the sense of Sahlins.) My point is just that the *"génie du paganisme"* [spirit of paganism] does not speak the theocratic language of belief. Pierre Clastres asked a good question: is it possible to conceive of a political power that is not founded on the exercise of coercion? All right, another is in order: is it possible to conceive of a religious form that does not root itself in the normative experience of belief? Perhaps this turns out to be exactly the same problem; but Clastres' reply was to invent Primitive Society, the quasi-transcendent subject of a non-coercive political power, while the response to the second question would imply a radical de-transcendentalization of this same subject.

Because of her insistence on the thesis of the incipient political centralism of the Tupi-Guarani—and thus on the revolutionary nature of the prophets, who questioned the dangerously pre-statist power of the great war chiefs—Hélène Clastres tended, I think, to minimize the data that suggests a certain inconstant skepticism on the Indians' part towards the *karaiba*. Nor does she seem to take into account the innumerable observations of the Jesuits and chroniclers on the "absence of a king," i.e. of strong political power with some trace of centralism, among the coastal Tupi. At the least, it should be noted that there may be deep differences between the Guarani of contemporary Paraguay and the coastal Tupi, or, to cite the author herself, "it is necessary to proceed prudently, since the homogeneity [...] of Tupi-Guarani culture obviously does not authorize the automatic attribution to the second group of characteristics that we know to be true of the first." (On political power among the Tupi of the coast, see Fausto.)

The core of the question lies in the idea that "the religious" is the royal road leading to the ultimate essence of a culture. Behind this assumption one can make out the Durkheimian idol, totality. The Belief of the tribe is belief in the Tribe, the impulse to contemplate and constitute the Whole. It is the being and the perseverance in being of the tribe. To doubt that savages worship such an idol is to cast suspicion on the idea of society as a reflexive and identitarian totality instituted through the foundational gesture of excluding an exterior. And it is not necessary to be postmodern (Heaven preserve us) to doubt it. Tupinambá religion, rooted in the warrior exocannibalism complex, projected a form in which the *socius* was constructed through relationship with the other, in which the incorporation of the other required an exit from oneself—the exterior was constantly engaged in a process of interiorization, and the interior was nothing but movement towards the outside. Such a topology did not know totality. Much less did it suppose any monad or identitarian core that could obsessively patrol its borders and use the exterior as a negative mirror for self-identity. Instead, society was, literally, a "lower limit of predation," the indigestible remnant: what moved it was its relationship to the outside. The other was not a mirror, but a destination.

I am not saying—to insist on this negative anthropology—that something like a religion may not have existed, or a cultural order, or a Tupinambá society. I am only suggesting that this religion was not framed in terms of the category of belief, that this cultural order did not base itself on the automatic exclusion of other orders, and that this society did not exist outside of an immanent relation with alterity. What I am saying is that Tupinambá philosophy affirmed an essential ontological incompleteness: the incompleteness of sociality, and, in general, of humanity. It was, in other words, an order where interiority and identity were encompassed by exteriority and difference, where becoming and relationship prevailed over being and substance. For this type of cosmology, others are a solution, before being—as they were for the European invaders—a problem. The myrtle has reasons that the marble cannot know.

Savage inconstancy nonetheless appeared, in Jesuit eyes, under the irritating light of venal interest. To believe or not to believe: this question, for the heathens, found its answer in the material advantages that might come:

> (from Grã:) This people, Father [Loyola], is not converted by talking about the things of faith, nor with reasons, nor words of preaching. [...] The approach of the Whites, to convert them, is to promise temporal conveniences without any news of the things of faith...

> (from Nóbrega:) And if they have given us some signs of goodness and some hope during these

six years that we have had relationships with them, what has most caused these things is interest and the hope of it that they have, not the fervor of faith that they might have in their hearts.

(from Anchieta:) It is true [...] that our catechumens gave us at the beginning great signs of faith and probity. But, since they are moved more by the hope of profit and by a certain vainglory than by faith, they have no firmness and easily, at the smallest opposition, they return to the vomit, having, above all, no fear of the Christians.

(from Nóbrega:) In one regard these are worse than all, that when they come to my tent, because of some fish-hooks that I have given them, I will convert all of them, and with other fish-hooks I will change and unconvert them, because they are inconstant, and true faith does not enter into their hearts...

If, at the beginning, the Jesuits rejected what they saw as pure spiritual harlotry, it did not take long for them to pragmatically resort to economic blackmail as a form of persuasion and control:

(from Pires:) Great is the envy that the heathens have towards the newly converted, because they see how favored these are by the governor and by other leading figures, and if we wanted to open the doors to baptism almost all of them would come, which we do not do unless we know they are fit for it, and that [they] come with devotion, and with contrition for the bad habits in which [they] were raised, and also so that they do not return to going backwards...

(from Correia:) I have told some of the Indian leaders of these parts some things about instructing the King to give them neither large nor small knives [...] and that he does it,

because it is not reasonable for the good things
that God created to be given to those who do not
know God, until meanwhile they all make themselves Christians [...] In these parts of S. Vicente,
as along the whole coast, the safest and most
firm route must be to place them in a situation of
necessity, so that they might clearly see that they
have no way to get the tools for their fields except
by becoming Christians.

In sum: the heathen were not only inconstant, but
also allowed themselves to be guided, in their ideological perambulations, by greed for worldly goods. Here
is another theme that achieved great popularity, in the
construction of the negative image of the Indian—a
flighty subject, capable of doing anything for a handful
of trinkets—and one that continues to haunt the night-
mares of many well-intentioned observers: anthropologists, indigenist advocates, progressive missionaries
who would like to see "their" Indians reject, in the
name of the higher values of native culture, the fish-
hooks with which they are, well, hooked. As a ratio-
nalization, it is common to take refuge in the thesis
of the technical superiority of European implements,
whose irresistible attraction corrodes the marble
of cultural pride and authenticity. Without casting
doubt on the quite palpable material advantages that
"large and small knives" offer to people unfamiliar
with metallurgy, I think this explanation expresses
a banal utilitarianism, and ends up validating judg-
ments like those of the Jesuits. The alternative possibility—taking indigenous "venality" and "frivolity"
as a strategic camouflage permitting the acquisition
of precious things (like metal implements, or tranquility) in exchange for irrelevant concessions (like
the soul, or the recognition of constituted powers)—
is not entirely wrong, but seems to me insufficient.
Certainly many indigenous peoples treated and treat

White people like *idiots savants* from whom they can extract marvelous objects in exchange for superficial gestures; and many others pay the price of verbal adherence so as to be left alone. But, on top of implying a static and reified conception of culture as something that must be preserved under layers of reflective varnish, this argument misses the point that in many cases the "concessions" were quite real, and that the introduction of European goods and values had profound effects on native social structures. The argument also forgets that the relationship with the invaders' paraphernalia, although inevitably guided by autochthonous cultural ends, is not always legible in terms of a self-enlightened instrumentalism. The argument ignores, above all, that the foreign culture was often envisaged in its entirety as a value to be appropriated and domesticated, as a sign to be taken up and practiced as such.

It is no mere dialectical pirouette to say that the Tupinambá were never more themselves than when they expressed their desire to "be Christians like us." When they declared their wish to convert, the possible practical advantages that they sought were submerged inside a *"calcul sauvage"* in which being like the Whites—and the being of the Whites—was a value up for grabs on the indigenous symbolic market. European implements, beyond their obvious utility, were also signs of the powers of exteriority, which it was necessary to capture, to incorporate, and to make circulate, exactly like the writing, the clothes, the ritual bowing gestures of the missionaries, the bizarre cosmology that they disseminated. Exactly, moreover, like the values contained in the person of one's devoured enemies: the Tupinambá always were a "consumer society." That which we might call the alloplastic or allomorphic impulse of the Tupi cannot be farther from the pathos of alienation or the mirroring of the Master and the Slave. It is the necessary counterpart to a generalized cannibalism, which distinguishes itself radically from the other-annihilating frenzy proper to imperialisms, Western or other. Efforts to interpret Tupian person-eating in the simplistic terms of an impulse to control the other (symbolically, politically, or whatever one wants to call it) neglect this double face and this double movement: to incorporate the other is to take on the other's alterity. In the Indians' typically inconstant style, to be sure. The Tupinambá idea of "becoming White and Christian" did not match up at all with what the missionaries wanted, as was demonstrated by the final recourse to the shock therapy of the *compelle intrare*.

II
How the Tupinambá Lost (the) War

The eschatological preaching of the priests coincided at certain points with native ideas: the immortality of the soul, separate afterlives based on the
kind of life lived on Earth, an apocalyptic conflagration. But a difference of principles emerged with
regard to the injunctions involved in Christian and
indigenous conceptions of the straight path. As we
heard Pindabuçu say, warfare and vengeance were
synonymous with being a proper man. The imperative of vengeance sustained the social machine of the
peoples along the coast: "since the Tupinambá are
very bellicose, all of their principles rest on how they
will make war against their opponents [*contrários*, lit.
contraries]." Here is, then, the opposite of indigenous

inconstancy. For if the Indians proved to be admirably constant in at least one area, and if towards anything they felt a "very sensitive sentiment [...] one that lasts them long," it was in all matters related to vengeance:

> (from Nóbrega:) They have wars with each other, namely, one nation against another nation, ten or fifteen or twenty leagues away, so that they are divided among themselves. [...] And all of their honor consists in two things, namely, in having many women and killing their opponents, and that is their happiness and desire [...] And they do not have war because of greed that they have [...] but only for hatred and vengeance...

> (from Rodrigues:) [C]alling all of their relatives to come and get vengeance – which is the greatest honor they have, because when one is at the end of his last days he asks for the flesh of his enemies to eat, because that way they go consoled, and also they take great honor in having at the head of the hammock, where they sleep, a pack of human flesh...

> (from Grã:) And what most blinds them, is the insatiable appetite that they have for vengeance, of which their honor consists...

> (from Anchieta:) [T]heir wars, in which they have placed almost all of their thought and care...

> (from Soares de Souza:) [Before leaving for war, a leader harangues them, speaking to them of the] obligation they have to go and exact vengeance on their adversaries, making clear to them the obligation they have to do it and to fight bravely; promising them victory against their enemies, without any danger on their part, that memory of them

will remain for those who come after singing their
praises...

If the peoples of Brazil had no idols for which
they died, they nonetheless died, and killed, for other
things: for their "inveterate habits." Herein lies the
reason why these formed the real obstacle, more than
the prophets. Warrior vengeance lay at the root of all
of the bad habits. Cannibalism, polygamy, drinking
sprees, the accumulation of names, honors; everything
seemed to turn around this theme. The discourse of
the *karaiba* may have preached the abolition of essential rules, suspending the social structure in favor of a
Turnerian *communitas*—the abandonment of matrimonial regulations, of agricultural village life. But note
that even this radical discourse preserved and encouraged the warrior enterprise. Let us recall the classic triad
of promises made by prophets: long life, abundance
without work, and victory over enemies. Shamanism
possessed decisive connections to war: the "Pagez and
Caraibes," Thevet said, "like oracles, predict the events
of their affairs, and especially wars, which is the people's
principal study;" "the greatest thing that the aforemen-
tioned Pagez ask of the spirit are things related to the
fact of war..."

The ruby thread of vengeance ran through the
life and death of Tupinambá men and women. At birth,
a male child received a small bow and arrow and a necklace of jaguar and harpy-eagle claws,

(from Thevet:) [S]o that he might be virtuous and
of great courage, as if to make him promise that he
will always make war against their enemies, all the
more so since this people never reconciles itself to

> those against whom they have had war in the past
> [...] If it is a girl, they place around her neck some
> teeth from a beast that they call *Capiigouare* [...]
> in order, they say, to make [her] teeth better and
> stronger for eating their meats...

Perhaps it is too much to suppose that "their meats"
refers to the flesh of captives, but the rites of menarche
involved the same placing of a necklace made from the
teeth of a capybara "so that [...] their teeth might be
stronger in order to chew their beverage that they call
Kaouin." This process seems to mark the two sexes for
their principal activities in the warrior complex: the
men responsible for the capture and killing of enemies,
the women for the production of an essential compo-
nent of the cannibal feast, the cauim, an intoxicating
beverage made from fermented manioc chewed by
female adolescents.

For the men, the rite of passage equivalent to
the menarche rites was the ceremonial execution of a
prisoner. Without having killed a captive and passed
through his first name change, a young man was not
fit to marry and have children. No mother would give
her daughter to a man who had not captured one or
two enemies and thus changed his childhood name.
The reproduction of the group, thus, was ideally
linked to the apparatus of capture and ritual execution
of prisoners, the motor of war. Once married, men
had to present their parents- and brothers-in-law with
captives, so that these affines could avenge themselves
and win new names; this matrimonial prestation seems
to have been one of the requirements for a man to exit
uxorilocal "servitude."

An alternative prestation involved the granting of a daughter to the wife's brother; the Tupinambá, as is well known, were ardent supporters of avuncular marriage. The failure to comply with these obligations might lead a brother to take his sister back. See the account by Vicente Rodrigues: "they had gone to war to avenge themselves, and a son of a Leader at the same Village also went, a Christian [...] named Bastián Téllez...; and having gone they killed and captured many opponents, and he captured one who was granted to him as his share. Since they had the victory, the relatives of the wife of Bastián Téllez asked for his captive, saying that if he did not give it to them, they would then have to take the wife, and he gave them the captive because of the shame he would receive in the eyes of the Whites if his wife were taken." On the granting of daughters as a condition for exiting uxorilocality, and on the young, recently married man's obligation to present his affines with captives, see Thevet.

As they captured and executed war captives, men accumulated names and fame:

(from Nóbrega:) Their happiness is to kill and to have names, and this is the glory for which they do the most...

(from Staden:) A man considers it his greatest honor to capture and kill many enemies, which is habitual among them. They have as many names as enemies they have killed, and the most noble among them are those who have many names.

(from Cardim:) Of all of the honors and enjoyments of life, none is as great for this people as killing and taking names on the heads of their adversaries, nor

are there among them any feasts that can rival those
that they hold for the deaths of those that they kill
with great ceremonies...

(from Monteiro:) One of the greatest appetites that
this nation has is the killing of enemies, for which
they go to extremes [...] in order to be considered
valiant, since among them it is the supreme honor
and happiness to take new names, in accordance
with the opponents they have killed, and some
manage to have one hundred and more names...

Such names—memories of feats of bravery,
signs and essential values of Tupinambá honor—made
up part of a full panoply that included scarifications,
facial piercings and plugs, the right to give speeches
in public, and the accumulation of wives. Sumptuary
polygamy seems to have been an attribute of chiefs or
great warriors. The accumulation of captives, of signs,
of women, of sons-in-law: escaping from uxorilocal
dependence through warrior fame, a man would be
capable of imposing this form of subjection on his
young sons-in-law, the husbands of daughters gener-
ated with his many wives: "and thus he who has
many daughters is honored by the sons-in-law that he
acquires with them, who are always subject to their
fathers- and brothers-in-law..."

Moreover, if warrior prowess was the condition of honor in this world, it was also necessary for a
comfortable existence in the Beyond: only the brave had
access to Paradise, the souls of cowards being destined
for miserable wandering about the Earth, along with
the Anhang devils. There is still more: if achieving
vengeance by killing enemies was the mark of a life of
valor, the *kalos thanatos* ["good death" T.N.] was that

suffered during combat, and, supremely, by being the victim of a ceremonial execution in the central square. Captivity and "sacrifice" were to be met with bravery and haughtiness:

> (from Azpicuelta:) This evil of eating each other has suffered great setbacks among them, so much so that some days ago they asked one or two, whom they were keeping to fatten up for this purpose, if he wanted to get rescued; he told them not to sell him, because he would comply with his honor by passing through such a death as a valiant captain.

> (from Blázquez:) They have persuaded their adversaries that in going through all of those ceremonies the adversaries are valiant and resolute, and then they call them weak and timid if they refuse to do this because of the fear of death; and as a result it happens that, in order to avoid such a reputation, which in their view would be very bad, they do things in the moment of dying that would seem unbelievable to those who have not seen them, because they eat and drink and take pleasure, like men without sense, in the joys of the flesh with such a leisurely manner that one thinks they have never heard of dying.

It would be hasty, of course, to conclude that Tupinambá war was guided solely, or even principally, by the goal of entering Paradise; recall that Pindabuçu did not mention the salvation of his soul as a reason for not violating the imperative of vengeance; rather, he simply affirmed the unthinkability of such a dereliction. His argument was absolute shame, not eternal perdition. There is no doubt that war had many religious connections, and that the Tupinambá were relatively fascinated with the theme of personal immortality; but I think it was more the case that they hoped to reach Heaven *because* they had followed the norms of warrior bravery, rather than following the norms *in order to* reach Heaven.

There are here two intertwined motifs, one of an eschatological and personal order, the other of a sociological and collective order. Being devoured by one's enemies was associated with a theme characteristic of Tupi-Guarani cosmologies, the horror of burial and of the rotting of the corpse:

> (from Anchieta:) Even the captives judge that what is happening to them in this situation is a noble and dignified thing, for them to stumble upon such a glorious death, as they judge it to be, for they say that it is a thing of the timid soul and not a thing of war to die in such a manner that one has to hold up in the grave the weight of the earth, which they judge to be very great.

> (from Cardim:) [And] some go around so happy with having to be eaten, that in no way will they consent to be rescued to serve [as slaves], because they say that it is a sad thing to die and to be foul-smelling and eaten by animals.

Jácome Monteiro, evoking the "omens of the heathen," tells that one of the things that made a warrior expedition desist from its pursuit was the rotting of the provisions that they carried:

> [I]f the meat after having been cooked acquires maggots, which very easily occurs because of the great heat of the land, and they say that just as the

meat has taken on maggots, in that same way their adversaries will not eat them, but will let them fill up with maggots after they kill them, which is the greatest dishonor that there is among these barbarians.

One can make out the complicity between captives and captors, which made a Tupinambá the best enemy of a Tupinambá. Furthermore, various aspects of the captivity and execution of enemies bear witness to an effort to transform the prisoner into a being in the image of the Tupinambá, if he were not already so: Europeans had body and face hair removed and were painted in native style (the case of Hans Staden); the captives had to dance, eat, and drink with their captors, and sometimes had to accompany them to war. Furthermore, the delivery of a wife to the captive, his transformation into a "brother-in-law," seems to me to require such an explanation, as a system for socializing the enemy. The Tupinambá wanted to be sure that the other they would kill and eat was fully defined as a man, who understood and desired what was happening to him.

There is no doubt that the phenomenon of death and consumption by one's enemies must be understood in the context of the pan-Tupi problematic of immortalization through the sublimation of the corruptible part of the person, and that Tupinambá exocannibalism was directly a funerary system. It is equally certain, however, that the Tupinambá did not devour their enemies out of pity, but for vengeance and honor. Here we come upon the sociological motive that seems fundamental to me, linking back to something perhaps more profound than that set of personological themes about rotting and incorruptibility—and more resistant than cannibalism to the proselytizing efforts of the missionaries. What the death of enemies and death at the hands of enemies made possible was nothing more and nothing less than the perpetuation of vengeance:

> (from Gandavo:) [And] after they thus manage to eat the flesh of their adversaries, their hatreds are confirmed forever, because they feel this insult very strongly, and thus they always go around seeking to avenge themselves of each other...

> (from Abbeville:) One must first of all know that they do not conduct war to preserve or extend the limits of their country, nor to enrich themselves with the spoils of their enemies, but only for honor and for vengeance. Whenever they judge that they have been offended by neighboring or non-neighboring nations, whenever they remember their ancestors or friends imprisoned and eaten by their enemies, they mutually excite themselves to war...

Death in foreign hands was an excellent death because it was a death that could be vindicated, that is, a justifiable death and one capable of being avenged; a death with meaning, productive of values and people. André Thevet expresses admirably the conversion of death's natural fatality into a social necessity, and this into a personal virtue:

> And do not think that the prisoner is shocked by this news [i.e. that he would soon be executed and eaten], since he has the opinion that his death is honorable, and that it is much better for him to die this way, than in his home from some contagious death; for (they say) one cannot take revenge on death, which offends and kills men, but one can well

avenge those who have been killed and massacred in the act of war.

Vengeance was thus not the simple fruit of the Indians' aggressive temperament, of their almost pathological incapacity to forgive and forget past offenses. ("And from this come these wars with no just cause, but simply from a fixed idea of vengeance, and from a bestial apprehension, which makes them bloody like this, in which they are so deeply plunged, that if a fly passes in front of their eyes, they would want to avenge themselves of it.") On the contrary, it was precisely the institution that produced the memory. A memory, in turn, that was nothing other than that relationship to the enemy through which individual death placed itself in service to the long life of the social body. Hence the separation between the individual share and the group share, the strange dialectic of shame and offense: to die in foreign hands was an honor for the warrior, but an insult to the honor of his group, and it imposed the requirement of an equivalent reply.

> Hence the repulsion that many captives felt at the idea of fleeing or being rescued by Europeans: "and some are even so brutish that they do not want to flee once they are kept as prisoners; because there was one who was already in the main square tied up and ready to suffer and they gave him life and he did not want it but rather that they kill him, saying that his relatives would not consider him brave, and that all would run from him; and from that it comes to pass that they do not think much of death; and when they are in that hour they do not take it into consideration nor show any sadness about the step." Also see Abbeville: "even if it may be possible for them to flee, given the liberty that they enjoy, they never do

it even though they know that they will be killed and eaten soon. And this is because, if a prisoner were to flee, he would be taken in his land for cuave eim, a wretch, a coward, and dead to his own through a thousand condemnations for not having suffered torture and death among his enemies, as if those of his nation were not strong and courageous enough to avenge him."

At the end of the day, it was the case that honor rested in being able to serve as the motive for vengeance, as a pledge of the preservation of society through one's own becoming. The mortal hatred that linked enemies was the sign of a mutual indispensability. Exocannibalism, this simulacrum, consumed individuals so that their groups could maintain that which was essential: their relationship to the other, vengeance as a vital *conatus*. Immortality was obtained through vengeance, and the search for immortality produced it. Between the death of enemies and one's own immortality lay the trajectory of every person, and the destiny of all.

Speaking of Time

The context in which one may best appreciate the mnemonic function of vengeance is in the ceremonial dialogue between the captive and his future killer. The sacrifice of the prisoner operated along two separate dimensions, one (anthropo-)logical and the other (anthropo-)phagical. The cannibal anthropology of the Tupinambá expressed itself, above all, in a dialogical anthropophagy, a solemn logomachy that opposed the protagonists in the ritual drama of the execution. This dialogue was the culminating point of the rite. It was this, let us note in passing, that made the Tupinambá famous, thanks to the chivalrous reading carried out in "Des cannibales," where Montaigne interprets it as an Hegelian-style combat for recognition, a struggle to the death carried out within the element of discourse.

In fact, the dialogue is marvelously apt for a reading in terms of warrior honor. But, apparently, apt for little else. The examples of such dialogues hint at no religious meanings, make no mention of divinities, carry no allusions to the posthumous fate of the victim. On the other hand, in these dialogues every voice speaks of something that has gone unnoticed by the commentators. They speak of time.

The dialogue consisted of a harangue by the killer, who would ask the captive if he were one of those who had killed members of the killer's tribe, and if he were ready to die; the killer would exhort the captive to fall like a brave man, "leaving behind a memory." The captive would reply proudly, declaring that he was a killer and a cannibal, evoking the enemies who had died in the same circumstances in which he now found himself. A ferocious version of the "acquiescent victim," he would demand the vengeance that would cut him down, and he would warn: kill me, for mine will avenge me; you will fall in the same manner.

There are a number of references to these dialogues —the majority, unfortunately, in free indirect style or in summarized glosses:

(from Nóbrega:) And one day before they kill him, they wash him entirely, and the next day they take him out, and put him in a central square tied at the waist with a rope, and one of them comes quite well dressed up, and makes a speech to him as his ancestors would. And once it is done, he who is about to die responds, saying that it is a quality of the valiant to not fear death, and that he also had killed many of theirs, and that now his relatives were left, who would avenge him, and other similar things.

(from Gandavo:) These ceremonies having been completed, he withdraws from him at some distance, and he begins to make a speech in a sort of homiletic style, telling him to prove himself very avid in defending his person, so that they might not dishonor him, or say that he killed a weak man, effeminate, and of little spirit, and that he should remember the valiant who died in that manner, at the hands of their enemies, and not in their hammocks like weak women, who were not born to win such honors with their deaths. And if the suffering one is a stout person, and not fainting at that point, as happens to some, he responds to him with much arrogance and daring, telling him to kill him very quickly, because he has himself done the same to many of his relatives and friends; however he also reminds him that just as they are taking vengeance for their deaths on him, in the same way his people will necessarily avenge him as brave men and they will do unto him and to his whole nation things in that same manner.

(from Staden:) Next he who will kill the prisoner takes up again the sacrificial club and says: "Yes, here I am, I want to kill you, for your people also killed and ate many of my friends." The prisoner responds to him, "When I will be dead, I will still have many friends who will know how to avenge me."

(from Léry:) "Are you not of the nation... that is an enemy to us? and have you not yourself killed and eaten our relatives and friends?"— He, more self-assured than ever, responded: "Pa che tantan, aiouca atoupavé, yes, I am very strong and I have truly knocked out and eaten several of them... Oh, I am not feigning it; oh, how bold I have been to attack and seize your people, whom I have eaten so many, many times." The executor added, "You, now being in our power, will be right away killed by me, then smoked and eaten by all of us here."—"Well then," came the reply to him, "my relatives will also avenge me."

(from Anchieta:) [B]ut I had little success, because he did not want to be a Christian, telling me that those whom we baptized did not die as brave people, and he wanted to die a famous death and prove his valor, in the main square tied with very long ropes around his waist, which three or four young men would hold well stretched out, he started to say, "Kill me, for you certainly have in me that of which you can avenge yourselves, since I ate so-and-so your father, this brother of yours, and that son of yours"—making a great deal out of the many that he had eaten belonging to those others, with such great enthusiasm and festivity, that it seemed more that he was going to kill the others than be killed.

(from Cardim:) [And] their brutality is such that, since they fear no evil other than that present one, they are as whole as if it were nothing, so to speak, worth exercising their forces over, because afterward they will say farewell to life saying that many may die, since many have died, and that beyond this thing here their brothers and relatives will be left to take vengeance for them, and in this way one prepares oneself to leave one's body, which is through all the honor of one's death.

(from Soares de Souza:) [A]nd since these captives see the hour arriving in which they must suffer, they begin to orate and speak boldly about themselves, saying that they are already avenged of those who will kill them, telling of great deeds and deaths that they inflicted upon the relatives of the killer, whom they threaten, along with all of the people of the village, saying that their relatives will avenge them.

The dialogue seemed to invert the positions of the protagonists. Anchieta was astonished: the captive "seemed more that he was going to kill the others than be killed." And Soares de Souza observes that other inversion, now a temporal one: the captives would say that they *already had vengeance* on the one who would kill them. The verbal combat told of the temporal cycle of vengeance: the victim's past was that of a killer, the future of the killer will be that of a victim; the execution would weld past deaths to future deaths, giving meaning to time. One can compare this discourse, spoken, as it were, only in the past and future tenses, with what H. Clastres says about the Guarani sacred songs:

[In that sacred language] the one who speaks is also, and at the same time, the one who listens. And, if he questions, he nonetheless knows that there is no other response than his own question indefinitely repeated... [...] It is a question that elicits no response. Or, rather, what the beautiful words seem to indicate is that the question and the answer are equally impossible. All one has to do is attend to the tenses and verbal forms: affirmation does not occur except in the past and in the future; the present is always the time of negation.

In the Tupinambá dialogue, on the contrary, the present is the time of justification, that is, of vengeance—of the affirmation of time. The ceremonial duet and duel indissolubly bind together the warrior's two temporal phases, which here respond and listen to each other, questions and answers being permutable. It is this very non-Rortyan conversation between captive and killer that renders possible a relationship between the past and the future. Only the one ready to kill and the one ready to die are effectively present, that is, alive. The ceremonial dialogue was the transcendental synthesis of time in Tupinambá society. The a priori category of vengeance imposed this double schematism, verbal and cannibal, which gave body to becoming. Before eating, a small talk was necessary—and these two acts *explicated* temporality, which emerged from inside the relation of mutual implication and reciprocal presupposition with the enemy. Far from serving as a mechanism for recuperating an original wholeness—which would involve a denial of becoming—the vengeance complex produced time, by way of this verbal agonism. The rite was the great Present.

A semiophagy, an eating of signs, "literally." As has already been noted, the maximum possible care was taken to insure that the one to be killed and eaten was a man, a being made of words, capable of promising, and endowed with memory. Endless details of the rite, culminating in the dialogue, bear witness to this effort to constitute the victim as a thoroughly human subject. Frank Lestringant, in a beautiful analysis of Montaigne's essay on the Tupinambá, detects there the reduction of cannibalism to a mere "economy of the word"—the concealment of the savage dimension so vividly present in the accounts of the chroniclers. Montaigne, Lestringant argues, seems to have spun a radically non-alimentary account of Tupinambá cannibalism. The French essayist would thus be anticipating the symbolic reading that would reappear in modern anthropology after a long hiatus marked by the naturalization of cannibalism, a tendency articulated already in the 16th century by the truculent and protein-oriented Girolamo Cardano, who appears as a sort of ancestor to Marvin Harris. But the way in which Lestringant characterizes Montaigne's "idealism" seems to me to express perfectly the dialogical moment of the Tupinambá rite. Allow me therefore to press his words into my service:

> the flesh of the prisoner who will be eaten is not, in any sense, a food: it is a sign [...] the cannibal act *represents* an extraordinary vengeance... [...] [T]his effort to discern, through the practices of the cannibal, the permanence of a discourse... [...] Without dwelling on the consequences of the massacre, Montaigne returns always to the challenge to honor, the exchange of injuries, that "warrior song" that the prisoner composes before his death. We end up, therefore, forgetting that the cannibal's mouth has teeth in it. Instead of devouring, the mouth limits itself to pronouncing.

Doubtlessly the cannibals' mouths had teeth, along with (equally-sharp) tongues, but Lestringant forgets that it was the Tupinambá themselves, not Montaigne, who separated the mouth that devoured from the mouth that pronounced: the killer was the only one not to eat the enemy's flesh. The ceremonial speech, the "representation" of vengeance, transformed the flesh that would be eaten into a sign. The dialogical cook could not take a taste.

What is the content of this memory instituted by and for vengeance? Nothing but vengeance itself, that is, a pure form: the pure form of time, to be unfolded among enemies. With due respects to the theory of Florestan Fernandes, I do not think that warrior vengeance was an *instrumentum religionis* that restored the integrity of the social body when it was threatened by the death of a member, thus making society once again coincide with itself, relinking it to the ancestors through the sacrifice of a victim. Neither do I believe that cannibalism was a process for "recuperating the substance" of the society's dead members, through the intermediation of the devoured body of the enemy. For the point was not to take vengeance because people died and needed to be rescued from the destructive flow of becoming; the point was to die (preferably in enemy hands) *in order to* bring vengeance into being, and thus bring into being a future. The dead members of a group were that group's nexus to its enemies, not the reverse. Vengeance was not a step back, but a move forward; the memory of past deaths, those of one's group and those of the others, advanced the production of becoming. War was not the handmaiden of religion, but rather the opposite.

The double endlessness of vengeance—an interminable process and a relationship that transcended its own limits—suggests that it was not one of those widespread machines for abolishing time. Rather, it was a machine to produce time, and to travel in time (which might be the only way to really abolish it.) A link to the past, no doubt; but also the generation of the future, through the great present of the ceremonial duel. Without vengeance, that is, without enemies, there would be no dead, but also no children, and names, and feasts. Thus it was not the recuperation of the memory of the group's departed that was in play, but the persistence of a relationship with enemies. *They* were the guardians of collective memory, since the group's memory—names, tattoos, speeches, songs—was the memory of the enemies. Far from counting as an obstinate affirmation of autonomy by the partners in this game (as Florestan would have it, and later Pierre Clastres), Tupinambá war of vengeance was the manifestation of an originary heteronomy, the recognition that heteronomy was the condition of autonomy. What kind of motive is vengeance, if not a way to acknowledge that "the truth of society" is always in the hands of others? Vengeance was not a consequence of religion, but the condition of possibility and final cause of society—of a society that existed for and through its enemies. Therefore, the task at hand is not simply to displace religion and its beliefs in favor of vengeance and its honors as the functional hypostasis of Totality. What Tupinambá warrior vengeance expressed, in its quality as cardinal value of the society, was a radical ontological incompleteness—a radically positive incompleteness. Constancy and inconstancy, openness and obstinacy, were the two faces of a single truth: the absolute necessity of an exterior relation, in other words, the unthinkability of a world without Others.

The Old Law

Vengeance was thus the base of the "old law" that the missionaries had to destroy. If religion *strictu sensu* was the domain in which the Indians opened themselves to the Christian message, war and its consequences was where they closed themselves; if they demonstrated "very weak memory for things of God," they displayed an elephantine memory for things of the enemy. The inconstancy lamented by the priests meant, invariably, a return to the practices of ritual execution of captives, and sometimes to cannibalism. The Apostle of Brazil [Anchieta, T.N.], for example, inveighed against one such stumble, that of the converted chief Tibiriçá, the great hope of the Jesuits of Piratininga (São Paulo). In the "general war" that in 1555 pitted the Tupiniquim against the Tupinambá, Tibiriçá took captives and wanted at any cost to kill them in the old style:

> In this way the pretend nature of his faith was demonstrated, which until then had been disguised, and he and all of the other catechumens fell and returned heedlessly to the old habits. Therefore one cannot hope to achieve anything in this whole land with regard to the conversion of the heathen, unless many Christians come here and [...] subject the Indians to the yoke of slavery and oblige them to find shelter in the banner of Christ.

This was one of the apples of the extended discord between Jesuits and colonists over the control of the Indians. The priests were not blind to the possible positive effects that intra-Tupi warmaking might have on European security and perhaps on catechesis.

There were Malthusian conjectures:

> (from Brás:) They are so many, and the land is so great, and they grow so much, that if they did not have continual war, and if they did not eat each other, they would not fit.

There were also more political arguments:

> (from Nóbrega:) [In Bahia] they now all go about disturbed by cruel wars. [...] And now is the most appropriate time to subject them all and impose on them whatever one might like...

> (from Anchieta:) [T]his war was the cause of much good for our old disciples, who are now forced by necessity to leave all of the dwellings into which they had scattered themselves and all gather themselves to Piratininga.

But the priests never sank to the level of making the sort of cold thanksgiving prayer that Gandavo offered, p.ex.:

> [A]nd since there are many of them God permitted that they be adversaries to each other, and that there be between them great hatreds and discords, because if things were not so the Portuguese would not be able to live in the land nor would it be possible to conquer such a great mass of people.

And at the end of the day, the priests opposed war because they knew its goals and consequences— continuation of the old habits:

> (from Rodrigues:) With the newly-converted Christians going alongside their other relatives to

war, which the Fathers prohibited them to do because it was to eat each other...

(from Pires:) The obstacles that blocked things from going in the way that we greatly desired were the continual and very cruel wars that the natives themselves wage against each other, and this was the principal obstacle to being able to get along with them, their lack of tranquility, and from there come the killings and they eat each other, which was very difficult to prohibit...

Because of this the Jesuits complained bitterly about the European inhabitants, who encouraged hostilities between Indians and made the cannibal abomination seem decent:

(from Blázquez:) To those Indians who will stay here close by the Christians, although they are forbidden to eat human flesh, one will not be able to get them to stop going to war and killing during it, and consequently they will eat each other, which might well be forbidden to these neighbors of the Christians, since they are frightened, but it is the common practice of all of the Christians to make them go to war and kill, and to lead them to this by saying that in this way they will be safer, which is an utter hindrance to their conversion, and for this reason and others the Fathers will not dare to baptize them, while this is not disposed of.

(from Nóbrega:) On all the coast it is generally believed, by large and by small, that it is a great service to Our Lord to make the heathen eat and fight with each other, and people have more faith in this than in the living God, and they say that in this consists the security of the land. [...] To the heathen they praise and approve eating one another...

(from Nóbrega:) For this reason a great murmuring was raised among the Christians, saying that they should be allowed to eat, that in this was the security of the land, not looking at the fact that, even for the good of the land, it is better for them to be Christians and to be subjected...

But the priests managed, finally, to get the Governors-General to require official permission for native wars, to punish the crime of cannibalism, and to define the terms of surrender imposed on defeated groups in the successive wars that the Portuguese incited:

(from Blázquez:) [T]hat they might not kill their adversaries except when they went to war, as all other nations are accustomed to do, and, if by chance they capture some, that they either sell them or use them as slaves.

(from Nóbrega:) The law, which must be given to them, is to prohibit them from eating human flesh and making war without permission from the Governor; to make them have only one wife, to clothe themselves since there is much cotton, at least after they become Christians, to take away from them the sorcerers... to make them live tranquilly without moving around to another place, unless it is among Christians, having lands distributed that are sufficient for them, and with these Priests of the Society to teach them doctrine.

This is Nóbrega's famous "civilizing plan," prompted by the devouring of Bishop Sardinha by the Caetés (1556), which led the Jesuits to endorse the doctrine of just war on the heathen. However, the Society's position on intra- Tupinambá wars differed from their position on wars incited against Indians by Europeans. In the latter case, the Society oscillated between condemnation and commendation. The condemnation was motivated as much by indignation at the atrocities that the colonists committed as by competition with them, since the colonists, by taking Indians prisoner, stole them away from settlement in missionary villages. The commendation appeared under the framework of just war and the *compelle intrare* motto. Even in this case, the war was supposed to be as official as possible, promoted or sanctioned by the Governor-General. (Moreover, the Jesuit attitude towards anti-indigenous war is connected to the even more complicated problem of the legitimacy of Indian enslavement, which we lack space to discuss here.)

See also:

(from Nóbrega:) [M]en de Saa [the third Governor-General of Brazil, from 1558 to 1572 (T.N.)] was able to overcome the opposition of all of the Christians in this land, which came about because they wanted the Indians to eat each other, because they counted on this for the security of the land and they wanted the Indians to flee from each other so that they might have slaves and they wanted to take lands from the Indians against reason and justice and tyrannize over them in every way, and they did not want them to come together to be taught doctrine [...] and other inconvenient things of this kind. All of this Men de Saa overcame, and I do not consider this victory to be any smaller than all of the others that Our Lord gave him; and he prohibited human flesh to the Indians as far as his power reached, meat which before they would eat around the city and sometimes inside it. He took the guilty and held them prisoner until they clearly recognized their error.

Through an implacable war *on* Indians, the technological-political apparatus of the Portuguese managed to finally tame the war *of* the Indians, removing it as an indigenous social end only to transform it into a means for the invaders' own political ends. And thus the Tupinambá lost (the) war, two times over.

The numerous Jesuit references to the encouragement that colonists gave to intra-Tupinambá hostilities raise the question of whether the extent and intensity of indigenous war might not have been greatly increased by the European invasion—in a direct and deliberate way. I think that this was in fact the case, at least in some parts of Brazil. But to go on from there to assert that the Tupinambá warfare pattern of the middle of the 16th century can be essentially explained through "contact with the West" (this is the general position that Ferguson, despite his provisos, ends up maintaining) is to travel too far. Such a journey is warranted only by the contemporary tendency to impute any problematic aspect of Amerindian societies—generally, any aspect not explainable in terms of practico-adaptive considerations—to the devastating effects of the "West." For all its well-meaning radicalism, this type of thinking ends up casting the Amerindians as passive toys of the inexorable logic of the State and of Capital, just as they are elsewhere thought of as unconscious agents of ecological reason: between history and nature, society vanishes.

Tupinambá war was an irreducible given of that society; it was its reflexive condition and its mode of being, which, if it gained some momentum through the introduction of foreign tools and materials and was sometimes exploited by the Europeans, did not get created by the latter. Furthermore, the importance of war in Tupinambá society cannot be measured by the number of deaths that it caused, nor is it easily explained through ecological considerations:

> [A]ll of this sea coast, 900 miles long, is inhabited by Indians who without exception eat human flesh; in this they feel such pleasure and sweetness that they often cover more than 300 miles when they go off to war. And if they capture four or five enemies, without taking care of anything else, they go home with great clamor and feasts and extremely copious wines, which they make out of roots; they eat them such that they do not lose even the smallest nail, and all of their lives they take glory in that admirable victory.

This passage allows us to introduce a caveat that becomes necessary in the face of some more or less recent arguments about indigenous war. I do not think that the Tupinambá sources corroborate in any manner whatsoever the sociobiological speculations (decorated with a dubious statistical apparatus) of Chagnon on Yanomami blood vengeance, the differential reproductive success of the killers, and so on. In what concerns the Yanomami, my position is one of unrestricted agreement with Albert and Lizot. As far as the Tupinambá are concerned, what we have said here about war and vengeance refers to what could be called the ideological order of that society, such as it can be apprehended through 16th-century accounts. The data does not permit any statistical estimate of the number of cases of "violent" death, ritual or not. Passages like Anchieta's, above, seem to indicate that the goal was not the extermination of enemies (and Brás' Malthusian conjecture, cited above, undoubtedly belongs in the domain of "just so stories.") The indigenous battles described by the chroniclers involved plenty of boasting and the exchange of insults and gestures, and there is not a single reference to carnage—except, of course, when one is referring to the wars of the Portuguese against the Indians.

The person of the prisoner, who might live for years among his enemies until his death was decided upon, was symbolically appropriated by a number of people: the captor, the women who welcomed and guarded him, the men to whom he was presented by the captor, the ritual killer. After being executed, the enemy was eaten by hundreds of people; one death alone could bring together several allied villages, who shared a sort of very thin soup, in which the enemy's flesh was diluted to practically homeopathic levels. Enemies' bodies were thus symbolically (although not always really) scarce, for an adversary was eaten to the last fingernail, as Anchieta said. With regard to the polygamy of the leaders and famous warriors, it is difficult to identify the real import of this ideal. I consider the Tupinambá situation to fit with no major problems into the category of "brideservice societies" proposed by Collier and Rosaldo, and it is thus possible that one might apply to the Tupinambá as well the observation that in this type of society the link between polygamy and proficiency in war was more ideological than objective. This being said, one can in no way ignore abundance of data that underlines the high value attributed to warrior prowess, the ubiquity of the theme of vengeance, the initiatory nature of homicide, and the connections between warfare and marriage. However that may be, although perhaps it would be appropriate to label the Tupinambá "extremely warlike," it would be very inappropriate to consider them particularly "violent." The chroniclers and the missionaries depict their daily life as one marked by a notable affability, generosity, and courtesy. And, as I observed above, their hatred for their enemies, and the entire captivity / ritual execution / cannibalism complex, were founded on an integral recognition of the opponent's humanity—which has nothing to do, of course, with any sort of "humanism."

The Juice of Memory

There is one element of the heathens' bad habits that warrants special emphasis: the central place in the warrior complex occupied by corn or manioc fermented beverages, the cauim. The meaning of fermented drinks in Amerindian cultures still waits for an interpretive synthesis. Such beverages are closely associated with the motif of cannibalism, and point towards the decisive importance of women in the symbolic economy of these cultures. The Tupinambá sources suggest, beyond this, a connection between drinking feasts and memory, more specifically the memory of vengeance. The Tupinambá drank to *not* forget, and therein lies the problem of the *cauinagens* [drinking feasts], greatly detested by the missionaries, who perceived these feasts' dangerous relationship with everything they wanted to abolish. We have already seen that Anchieta considered one of the obstacles to the conversion of the heathens to be "their wines, which they drink very regularly, and which ordinarily can be taken away from them only with more difficulty than anything else..." It was harder to get rid of the "wines" than to get rid of cannibalism. But drinking feasts always raised the specter of that latter abomination:

> (from Jácome:) Their pleasures are how they must go to war, how they must drink for a day and a night, always drinking and singing and dancing, always on foot running all around the Village, and how they must kill their opponents and hold a new event for the killing; they must prepare themselves for their wines and their cooking of human flesh;

and their holy ones, who tell them that the old women will thereby become young girls...

(from Anchieta:) [B]ecause this people is so untamed and bestial, that they find all of their happiness in killing and eating human flesh, from which by the grace of God we have separated them; and with all of them the habit of drinking and singing their heathen songs is so deeply rooted, that there is no way to separate them from all of these things.

(from Grā:) And what has them most blind is the insatiable appetite they have for vengeance, of which consists their honor, and along with this the great amount of wine they drink, made out of roots or fruits, which must be entirely chewed by their daughters and other girls, who alone are used for this task while they are virgins. I do not know any better likeness of Hell than to see a crowd of them when they drink, because for this they invite people from very far away; and this especially when they have to kill someone or eat some human flesh, which they treat by roasting and smoking.

(from Azpicuelta:) From here I went full of sadness to other villages, where I also told them things about Our Lord. They took pleasure in hearing them, but then they forget them, shifting their attention back to their wines and wars.

(from Anchieta:) I return to our people, who are divided into three habitations so that they can drink freely, because this habit, or, to put it better, this nature, will have to be extirpated from amongst them with great difficulty, and if this remains it will not be possible to plant in them the faith of Christ.

The Jesuit attitude towards drinking recalls modern discourses that depict drugs as the source of all evils and crimes, with the particularity that the Tupinambá *cauinagens* were an intoxication through memory. Drunk, the Indians forgot the teaching of Christian doctrine and remembered what they should not. Cauim was the elixir of inconstancy:

> (from Anchieta:) These catechumens of ours, with whom we occupy ourselves, seem to distance themselves a little from their old habits, and now only rarely can one hear the tuneless shouts that they used to make during the drinking feasts. This is their greatest evil, from which all of the others flow. In fact, when they are the most drunk, the memory of their past evils becomes new again, and beginning to puff up with pride they soon burn with the desire to kill enemies and with hunger for human flesh. But now, since the heedless passion of the drinks has decreased a little, the other nefarious ignominies have necessarily also decreased; and some are so obedient to us that they do not dare to drink without our permission, and only in great moderation if we compare it with the former insanity [...] However, this consolation of ours is diminished by the obstinate hardness of the parents, who, excepting some, seem to want to return to the vomit of old habits, going to parties with their most miserable singing and wines, on the occasion of the upcoming killing of an [opponent] that was being readied in a neighboring village.

Jácome Monteiro tersely explains the presentifying function of the *cauinagens*, in their relationship with the "oral complex" of the songs, the declaration of brave deeds, and the pronouncement of names:

[T]aking new names, in accordance with the opponents they have killed, some come to have a hundred and more names, and in telling about these they are very detailed, because during all the wines—that is the greatest feast of these heathen— they recount the way they achieved these names, as if it were the first time that such a deed had happened; and as a result there is no child who does not know the names that each one has achieved, killing enemies, and this is what they sing and tell. However the gentlemen never make mention of their names, except when there is a feast of wines, in which one only hears about the practice of war, how they killed, how they entered the stockade of the enemy, how they broke their heads. Alongside the wines come the memories and tales of their deeds.

See also Soares de Souza on homicide, name-giving, and drinks:

It was the habit, among the Tupinambá, that anyone who had killed an opponent would soon take a name amongst them, but he does not say it until the right moment, when he orders great wines to be made; and since the wines are about to be ready for drinking, they dye themselves the day before with genipap [the fruit of *Genipa americana*, used for dyeing skin black (T.N.)], and they begin in the afternoon to sing, and all night long, and after they have sung for a great stretch, all of the people of the town go around begging the killer to tell them what name he took, for which he makes them beg him, and as soon as he says it, they prepare new songs, based on the killing of the one he killed, and on praises of him, the killer...

We are here, once again, faced with what might be called the "oral" complex of the Tupinambá: the enormous prestige of the singers and the "masters of speech," the marking with facial piercings and lip plugs of the right to speak in public, the ritual conferring of names, et cetera. Jácome Monteiro: "Just as the second blessing among them is to be singers, the first is to be killers." The indigenous custom of boasting about feats of bravery with endless speeches greatly irritated the Europeans.

Finally, it should be remembered that an individual could only start drinking cauim after having killed an enemy, or having married—therefore, those who drank were killers and women who had passed through the puberty rite. That explains observations like the following:

(from Grã:) For the children we have much hope, because they have skill and intelligence, and if taken before they go to war, to which they go, and the women as well, and before they drink and understand impure things...*

(from Grã:) [T]he men up to 18 and 20 years present good signs, from then on they begin to drink and they make themselves so coarse and so terrible that it is unbelievable. This is the sin that they seem least likely to improve, because the time when they are not drunk is very little, and in those wines, when they do all of those things, they speak of all evil things and dishonesties...

---

*This passage is difficult to translate, and admits of several possible interpretations. After consultation with Prof. Viveiros de Castro, I have settled on the version presented above. The original is as follows: "De los niños tenemos mucha esperança, porque tienen habilidad y ingenio, y tomados ante que vaian a la guerra, ado van y aún las mujeres, y antes que bevan y entendian en desonnestidades."

And it also explains the priests' pride when the children living in the schools took initiatives like that described by Pero Correia:

> [A]nd there are some of these youngsters [of the school of Piratininga] so lively and so good and so daring that they break the jars full of wine belonging to their own people, so that these might not drink.

Recalcitrant Cannibals

We come, finally, to the question of the abandonment of cannibalism. We saw how Nóbrega's first letter, as well as Pindabuçu's discussion with Thevet, suggested that the Tupinambá seemed ready to leave behind the cannibal element of their warrior system in exchange for health, long life, and other benefits promised by the priests—but that that the wars of vengeance, as such, remained untouchable.

We have transcribed passages from letters and other chronicles that attest to the importance of cannibalism as the perfect and fully-achieved form of vengeance, crowning a ritual system that involved the capture, captivity, and execution of enemies. There are numerous other references to the difficulty of rescuing enemies from the hands of their Indian captors, to the violent opposition to baptism *in articulo mortis* ["at the moment of death" T.N.] (it ruined the meat, as we have already noted), and to the tactics employed by the Tupinambá in order to eat their opponents against the prohibitions of the priests. But the letters also reveal a certain ambiguity on the part of the Indians when they were faced with the scandalized arguments of the missionaries, an attitude that hesitated between firmness and washing one's hands:

> (from Azpicuelta:) [They are] very deeply rooted in the eating of human flesh, so much so that, when they are crossing out of this world, they then ask for human flesh, saying that they can have no consolation but this, and if one is not able to find it for them, they say that they are going as the most disconsolate men in the world; the consolation is their

vengeance. Most of my time I spend reproaching them for this vice. The response that some give me is that only old women eat. Others say to me that their grandparents ate, that they must also eat, for it is their habit to take vengeance in that manner, since their opponents ate them: and why do I want to take away their true and proper delicacy?

Even among the Tamoio of Iperoig, little subjected to the Europeans and still outside the reach of Jesuit indoctrination, Anchieta found that his anti-cannibal message did not fall on deaf ears:

> [I admonished them]... especially that they should loathe the eating of human flesh because that way they would not lose their souls in Hell, where all eaters of it go and those who do not know God their Creator, and they promised us to never again eat it, demonstrating much regret that their ancestors had died without this knowledge and been buried in Hell. Some women in particular said the same thing, and they seemed to rejoice most of all in our doctrine, and they promised that they would do thus; to the men in general we spoke of this, telling them how God prohibits it, and that we in Piratininga do not allow those we teach to eat them nor anyone else, but they said that they would still eat their opponents, until they had avenged themselves well on them, and that they would slowly fall into our habits, and it is true, because the habit in which they have put their greatest happiness cannot be torn away from them so quickly, although it is the case that there are some of their women who never ate human flesh, nor eat it now; before the moment when someone is killed, and they make a feast in the place, these hide all of their cups that they employ to eat and drink, so that the others

might not make use of them, and along with this there are other habits so naturally good that they seem to have not originated in a such a cruel and bloody nation.

In truth, if some of these letters depict Indians who say that human flesh is their "true and proper delicacy," like that of Azpicuelta above, or this one from Blázquez—

[J]ust as some place their joy in money or sensual contentment, or in being valiant, in that same way these heathen have placed their happiness in killing an opponent and afterward, out of vengeance, eating his flesh, so much without horror and disgust that there is no delicacy, in their taste, that can match this one...

—nonetheless others, like that of Anchieta above, indicate that cannibalism was not exactly a matter of unanimity. The Apostle of Brazil would repeat this years later: "All of those on the coast who have a common language eat human flesh, although some in particular have never eaten it and have a very great disgust for it." It is in this same document, moreover, that one can find that list of the impediments to conversion that we presented at the beginning of this essay. One should note that Anchieta's list already did not include cannibalism as one of the impediments. By that point, among the Indians under the control of the Jesuits and the colonists, Indian war had already been completely subordinated to the ends of the invaders, or was carried out in the minimalist form of vengeance without a cannibal feast. In French Maranhão, during the first years of the following century, Abbeville would find the same apparent physical repugnance for cannibalism, which was practiced almost as an obligation:

> It is not exactly pleasure that leads them to eat such morsels, nor the sensual appetite, since I have heard from many that not uncommonly they vomit it after eating, because they do not have stomachs capable of digesting human flesh; they do it only to avenge the death of their ancestors and to satisfy the invincible and diabolical hatred that they devote to their enemies.

It does not seem easy to reconcile these reports of repulsion towards cannibalism, and of a certain disposition to cease it, with other reports that affirm its value and honor—and even its excellence as an alimentary practice—like the extremely famous dialogue of Hans Staden with the leader Cunhambebe:

> During this Cunhambebe had in front of him a large basket full of human flesh. He was eating from a leg; he held it for me in front of my mouth and asked me if I would like to eat as well. I responded: "An irrational animal would not eat another of its kind, and should a man devour another man?" He then bit it and said, "*Jauára iché.* I am a jaguar. It's delicious." I withdrew from him, having seen this.

A question of cultural taste, some might say. The problem is that in the Tupinambá case opinions, it seems, varied *inside* the group. Above all, even those who heartily praised this eating and this food came to leave such practices behind with relative ease. Everything suggests, at any rate, that the practice of cannibalism had a differentiated weight in the warrior system of the

Tupi and Guarani of the coast. The Tupinambá of Bahia, for example, appear to have held on with special tenacity; the Tupiniquim of São Paulo allowed themselves to be dissuaded more easily; and the Carijó (Guarani) of the southern coast seem to have been, perhaps, even less given over to cannibalism.

To explain the abandonment of cannibalism by the Indians—or, rather, to determine the motives and processes responsible for the greater ease with which this practice was restricted by the Jesuits and Governors-General, in comparison to the wars of vengeance—we would need to conduct a global analysis of the meaning of cannibalism in Tupian cultures. That is something we do not here attempt. We have already mentioned one aspect of the cannibal's motivation, that which envisages the situation from the victim's perspective: the avoidance of burial and rot, or, in other words, a method for "making the body lighter," an important theme in Tupi-Guarani theories of the person. Approaching things the other way around, from the perspective of the eaters, cannibalism allows several connections to appear. First of all, it was the aspect and mode of vengeance appropriate to the collectivity of the captors and their allies (while, by contrast, the ritual execution was carried out by only one man, who did not eat the opponent's flesh). In this sense, it amounted to the maximal socialization of vengeance, through which all of the eaters affirmed themselves as the enemies of the enemies, placing themselves inside the field of "compulsory revenge" in the eyes of the collective associated with the victim. Moreover, there are suggestions that cannibalism linked back to the same eschatological and personological themes that cut across the religion, shamanism, and mythology of the Tupi-Guarani. The repeated references to the voracity of old women—the great enemies of the Jesuits in the matter of the extirpation of cannibalism—suggest that the object sought in the cannibal meal must have been no different from that which the *karaiba* promised: "And promise them long life, and that the old women will definitely become young girls..." Cannibalism seems to have been, among many other things, the specifically female method for obtaining long life, or even immortality, which in the masculine case was obtained through bravery in combat and courage at the final hour. See the passage by Azpicuelta already cited: "The response that some give me is that only old women eat..." (There is much more here than a mere ideological ghost projected by the European observers, as Bucher thinks.) There are even hints that human flesh directly produced that lightening of the body that the Tupi-Guarani sought in so many different ways: through shamanic asceticism, dance, or the ingestion of tobacco (see Combès, and Saignes, cited by her.) Furthermore, the cannibal rite was a carnivalesque staging of ferocity, a becoming-other that revealed the paradoxical impulse behind Tupinambá society—when absorbing the enemy, the body social became, in the rite, determined by the enemy, constituted by the enemy.

The maximum form of vengeance, cannibalism was nonetheless not its necessary form. The gesture that characterized warrior vengeance, and the crucial requirement for the attainment of a new name, was the ritual shattering of the adversary's skull:

> (from Brandão:) [E]ven if this heathen in the field kills the enemy by stabbing... since he did not kill him by breaking his head, they immediately think that the dead man is not dead, nor can the killer

boast of having brought him to death, nor can he take a name nor get himself marked.

Sometimes, enemies were exhumed to split their heads:

> (from Anchieta:) [S]ince they are not content with killing the dead, but they also exhume the dead and want to break their heads for greater vengeance and to take a new name.

> (from Soares de Souza:) [I]f they find some old grave of the enemies, they exhume the skull, and break it, upon which they take a new name, and newly become enemies.

This gesture was an exclusively masculine one. Women could kill a prisoner with their own hands, when enraged; but they needed to call a man to break the skull of the body.

Vengeance in its minimal and necessary form—confrontation with an enemy to break his skull, preferably in the ritual situation—proved more resistant than cannibalism to Jesuit injunctions. This fact was probably due to the indispensability of vengeance in the process of producing complete masculine persons, renowned and re-named killers. Doubtlessly, the fact that anthropophagy was an absolute abomination, while vengeance was merely a "bad habit," must have also inclined the Europeans to treat the latter with more tolerance. It may be possible, at any rate, to see in the abandonment of cannibalism a defeat primarily for the female section of Tupinambá society.

How easy was it to dissuade the Tupinambá from eating their enemies? In Bahia, it required a campaign of wars, sometimes wars of extermination

(Itapoã, Paraguaçu), directed by the Governors-General, which ended with the prohibition of indigenous wars without permission, and with the decree of the death penalty for the crime of anthropophagy. The Indians submitted themselves with death in the soul:

(from Blázquez:) [The leader Tubarão (Shark) goes to war]: He asked the Governor for permission to kill that one, for that one was one of those who had killed his people, in order to console the disgust he felt on account of those of his that had died. The Governor gave him permission for them to kill the prisoner outside of the Village. Thus they did it, and they killed him and ate him, for he was found being cooked. [Upon the protests of the priests, the governor, Duarte da Costa] ordered it to be announced throughout his Villages under pain of death that no-one eat human flesh, so that the Indians had great fear struck into them.

(from Blázquez:) This contract became hard for the Indians, because, just as some place their joy in money or sensual contentment, or in being valiant, in that same way these heathen have placed their happiness in killing an opponent and afterward, out of vengeance, eating his flesh, so much without horror and disgust that there is no delicacy, in their taste, that can match this one: and this was the cause for which they told the Governor that by taking this away from them he had taken away all of the glory and honor that their elders had left them, but, however, that they were prepared from then on to no longer do that which we hated so much, on the condition that they be allowed now to kill seven adversaries whom they had held for a long time in ropes in order to eat them, claiming that these had killed their parents and their children. The

Governor granted their wish, except that they not eat the captives, and thus they promised, a thing that they would never do, nor would they have ever done this if we had not put them in such a difficult position, because they do not consider themselves avenged through just killing them, but through eating them.

But they ended up submitting, and then cannibalism was nothing but an ashamed memory:

(from Pires:) All of these are losing the practice of eating human flesh, and, if we know that some have it to eat and we send a message asking them for it, they send it to us, as they did in recent days and they brought it to us from very far away so that we might bury it or burn it, in such a way that all tremble with fear of the Governor...

(from Nóbrega:) The human flesh that all ate—and very close to the city—is now taken away, and many already take it as an insult to recall that time, and if in some place they eat it they are censured and punished for this.

(from Pires:) [A]nd that they must neither kill nor eat human flesh: that was superfluous because already they now are not doing that.

(from Pereira:) All tell me that it is very easy for us to do away with them since they do not eat human flesh...

In the south, among the Tupinquim of São Vicente and Piratininga, the Jesuits seem to have achieved success more quickly in their efforts at dissuasion:

> (from Anchieta:) It is also a great thing to marvel at and for which to give much thanks to the all-powerful God, that both these ones and the others in neighboring places who have now heard of us for some time, and even now often hear the word of God, do not eat human flesh, since they do not have any subjection nor fear of the Christians.

Even the occasional slips among the catechumens, which repeatedly led Anchieta to cry out for "the preaching of the sword and of the iron rod," did not feature this practice:

> [They are] totally immersed in their old and diabolical habits, except the eating of human flesh, which, through the goodness of the Lord, seems that it has been somewhat uprooted amongst them whom we have taught. It is true that they still hold great feasts upon the killing of their enemies, they and their children, even those who know how to read and write, drinking great wines as used to be their custom, and, if they do not eat them, giving them to others to eat, to their relatives who come from various places and are invited to the feasts. All of this comes because they are not subjected...

An essential tool in the struggle against cannibalism—perhaps the decisive stroke—was the internment of Indian children in Jesuit schools, with the very probable inculcation of a sacred horror at that practice:

> (from Nóbrega:) [B]ecause although many young ones go backwards to follow the habits of their fathers where there is no subjection, at least this is gained, that they do not return to eating human flesh, but rather banish it from their parents...

There would be a whole different study to be done on the Jesuit strategy of kidnapping Tupinambá children.

In praise of inconstancy

Tupinambá sources seem, in closing, to justify Lévi-Strauss' observations on the lability of cannibalism. Where the practice exists, says the author, it is rarely coextensive with the social body, and even

> there where the practice seems to be the norm, one may note exceptions in the form of reticence or repugnance. The labile character of cannibal customs is striking. In all of the available observations, from the 16th century until the present, we see these customs emerge, spread, and disappear in a very short period of time. It is this, doubtlessly, that explains cannibalism's frequent abandonment after the first contacts with Whites, even before these Whites possessed coercive means.

In the Tupinambá case, cannibalism did coincide with the entire social body: men, women, children —all had to eat the adversary. In fact, it was he who constituted this body in its maximum density and extension, at the moment of the cannibal feasts. This practice, however, demanded an apparently minor and temporary exclusion, but one that proved decisive: the killer could not eat his victim. This seems to me to amount to more than a mere application of that widely-diffused principle in indigenous America, namely, the principle that forbids the hunter from eating his catch. The abstinence of the killer points towards a division of labor in the rite of execution and ingestion—a division in which, while the community transformed itself into a ferocious and bloody mob, while it staged a becoming-animal (recall the jaguar of Cunhambebe) and a becoming-enemy, the killer was the one who carried the burden of rules and the symbolic. Immediately after killing his opponent he entered into a rigorous seclusion, a classic liminal state, preparing himself to receive a new name and a new social personality. He and his dead enemy were, in a certain sense, the only proper human figures in the entire ceremony. Cannibalism was possible because one did not eat.

We have also seen that, despite its multiple religious connections and its cosmological and eschatological meanings, cannibalism was not the *sine qua non* of the system of warrior vengeance, but rather its ultimate form. We have seen, further, that some sources attest to the existence of movements of repulsion against the eating of human flesh. We have observed that, in at least some parts of Brazil, cannibalism was abandoned through no more than Jesuit preaching, before any possibility of military pressure. And we noted, in conclusion, that cannibalism does not seem to have persisted past the 1560s among the Tupinambá in direct contact with Europeans.

Lévi-Strauss takes cannibalism as an unstable figure traced out against the background of a fundamental identification to the Other, a background that would be something like the general condition of social life. Cannibalism would be located at the extreme point on a gradient of sociability, whose other pole would be indifference or incommunicability: cannibalism would express an *excess* of sociability, not a total lack thereof. If this is the case, then the abandonment of such a practice would mean, in some way, the loss of an essential dimension of Tupinambá society: its "identification" with enemies, that is to say, its self-determination through the Other, its condition of perpetual *alteration*.

But then at the same time, one might ask if the relative speed with which cannibalism was abandoned could not in fact be attributed to the arrival of the Europeans. Might this abandonment have occurred not only or principally because Europeans hated and repressed cannibalism, but rather because they came to occupy the place and the function of the enemy in Tupian society? They filled in that "exterior" space to such an extent that the values they conveyed, and which had to be incorporated, ended up eclipsing the values that were interiorized through the eating of traditional enemies. The persistence of warrior vengeance, and of its consequences for the whole complex of names, honors, and memories, bears witness to the extent to which the fundamental motif of ontological predation remained with the Tupinambá for some time still. It also bears witness—and so does the ethnology of contemporary Amerindians—to the fact that one does not have to literally eat the others in order to continue depending on them as sources for the very substance of the social body, a substance that was nothing more than this cannibal relation to alterity. At any rate, if cannibalism is in fact a labile and unstable form *par excellence*—I almost said "inconstant"—then it could not have been more emblematic of the Tupinambá, a people admirably constant in their inconstancy.

The Araweté, a small, contemporary Tupian people in eastern Amazonia, claim—I do not know if they believe—that the *Maï*, a race of celestial divinities, are cannibals. The *Maï* devour the souls of the dead who have recently arrived in Heaven; then they immerse the remains in a magic bath that resurrects and rejuvenates the dead, transforming them into immortal beings like themselves, who live in a perfumed paradise where abound drink, sex, and music. The only souls who do not need to endure this celestial cannibalization are those belonging to men who killed an enemy in life. Feared by the *Maï*, Araweté killers are already like them, ferocious and cannibalistic (it is thought that a murderer has a stomach filled with the blood of the enemy, and must purge it). Thus they do not need any god to digest for them a humanity they have already left behind. The *Maï*, who abandoned the earth at the beginning of time, are not conceived as fathers, creators, or even culture heroes for humans. In truth, they are classified as "our huge *tiwã.*" *Tiwã*, a word of joking-aggressive connotations, means "potential affine," and it is in this way that the spirit of a dead enemy calls to his killer, in dreams, to teach him songs. In sum: these celestial cannibals, who devour us to transform us into something in their image and (non) resemblance, are the enemies and potential affines of humans, but also represent an ideal for us. From the Tupian cannibal sociology of the 16th century, the Araweté developed an eschatology no less cannibal. Enemies transformed themselves into gods, or, rather, we humans now occupy the place of the enemies, while we hope to be, through death, transformed into our enemies/ affines, the gods. The *Maï* are, somehow, the old Tupinambá transformed into gods. As one can see, the inconstant soul of the Tupi remains implicated in cannibal affairs. ■

Acknowledgements

I thank Marcio Goldman, Tânia Stolze Lima, and Carlos Fausto for the discussions that led to the final version of this essay, and especially Manuela Carneiro da Cunha, for her partnership in formulating, many years ago, much of that which is here expressed (cf. Carneiro da Cunha & Viveiros de Castro 1985.) The essay was written thanks to the generous insistence of Aurore Becquelin and Antoinette Molinié, who waited for it with patience and (in Aurore's case) translated it in part for publication in the collection *Mémoire de la tradition* (Becquelin & Molinié eds., 1993).

Also available from Prickly Paradigm Press:

continued